OTTO
VON
BISMARCK

OTTO VON BISMARCK

Jonathan E. Rose

CHELSEA HOUSE PUBLISHERS

NEW YORK

NEW HAVEN   PHILADELPHIA

EDITOR-IN-CHIEF: Nancy Toff
EXECUTIVE EDITOR: Remmel T. Nunn
MANAGING EDITOR: Karyn Gullen Browne
COPY CHIEF: Perry Scott King
ART DIRECTOR: Giannella Garrett
PICTURE EDITOR: Elizabeth Terhune

Staff for OTTO VON BISMARCK:

SENIOR EDITOR: John W. Selfridge
ASSISTANT EDITORS: Maria Behan, Pierre Hauser, Kathleen McDermott, Bert Yaeger
COPY EDITORS: Gillian Bucky, Sean Dolan
DESIGN ASSISTANT: Jill Goldreyer
PICTURE RESEARCH: Diane Wallis
LAYOUT: Ghila Krajzman
PRODUCTION COORDINATOR: Alma Rodriguez
COVER ILLUSTRATION: Richard Martin

CREATIVE DIRECTOR: Harold Steinberg

Frontispiece courtesy of AP/Wide World Photos

First Printing

Library of Congress Cataloging in Publication Data

Rose, Jonathan. OTTO VON BISMARCK

(World leaders past & present)
Bibliography: p.
Includes index.
1. Bismarck, Otto, Fürst von, 1815–1898—Juvenile
literature.   2. Prussia (Germany)—Politics and
government—1815–1870—Juvenile literature. 3. Germany—
Politics and government—1871–1888—Juvenile
literature.   4. Statesmen—Germany—Biography —Juvenile
literature I. Title. II. Series.
DD218.R67   1987   943.08′092′4 [B] [92]   86-29900

ISBN 0-87754-510-3

Contents

ADENAUER

ALEXANDER THE GREAT

MARC ANTONY

KING ARTHUR

ATATÜRK

ATTLEE

BEGIN

BEN-GURION

BISMARCK

LÉON BLUM

BOLÍVAR

CESARE BORGIA

BRANDT

BREZHNEV

CAESAR

CALVIN

CASTRO

CATHERINE THE GREAT

CHARLEMAGNE

CHIANG KAI-SHEK

CHURCHILL

CLEMENCEAU

CLEOPATRA

CORTÉS

CROMWELL

DANTON

DE GAULLE

DE VALERA

DISRAELI

EISENHOWER

ELEANOR OF AQUITAINE

QUEEN ELIZABETH I

FERDINAND AND ISABELLA

FRANCO

FREDERICK THE GREAT

INDIRA GANDHI

MOHANDAS GANDHI

GARIBALDI

GENGHIS KHAN

GLADSTONE

GORBACHEV

HAMMARSKJÖLD

HENRY VIII

HENRY OF NAVARRE

HINDENBURG

HITLER

HO CHI MINH

HUSSEIN

IVAN THE TERRIBLE

ANDREW JACKSON

JEFFERSON

JOAN OF ARC

POPE JOHN XXIII

LYNDON JOHNSON

JUÁREZ

JOHN F. KENNEDY

KENYATTA

KHOMEINI

KHRUSHCHEV

MARTIN LUTHER KING, JR.

KISSINGER

LENIN

LINCOLN

LLOYD GEORGE

LOUIS XIV

LUTHER

JUDAS MACCABEUS

MAO ZEDONG

MARY, QUEEN OF SCOTS

GOLDA MEIR

METTERNICH

MUSSOLINI

NAPOLEON

NASSER

NEHRU

NERO

NICHOLAS II

NIXON

NKRUMAH

PERICLES

PERÓN

QADDAFI

ROBESPIERRE

ELEANOR ROOSEVELT

FRANKLIN D. ROOSEVELT

THEODORE ROOSEVELT

SADAT

STALIN

SUN YAT-SEN

TAMERLANE

THATCHER

TITO

TROTSKY

TRUDEAU

TRUMAN

VICTORIA

WASHINGTON

WEIZMANN

WOODROW WILSON

XERXES

ZHOU ENLAI

ON LEADERSHIP
Arthur M. Schlesinger, jr.

LEADERSHIP, it may be said, is really what makes the world go round. Love no doubt smooths the passage; but love is a private transaction between consenting adults. Leadership is a public transaction with history. The idea of leadership affirms the capacity of individuals to move, inspire, and mobilize masses of people so that they act together in pursuit of an end. Sometimes leadership serves good purposes, sometimes bad; but whether the end is benign or evil, great leaders are those men and women who leave their personal stamp on history.

Now, the very concept of leadership implies the proposition that individuals can make a difference. This proposition has never been universally accepted. From classical times to the present day, eminent thinkers have regarded individuals as no more than the agents and pawns of larger forces, whether the gods and goddesses of the ancient world or, in the modern era, race, class, nation, the dialectic, the will of the people, the spirit of the times, history itself. Against such forces, the individual dwindles into insignificance.

So contends the thesis of historical determinism. Tolstoy's great novel *War and Peace* offers a famous statement of the case. Why, Tolstoy asked, did millions of men in the Napoleonic wars, denying their human feelings and their common sense, move back and forth across Europe slaughtering their fellows? "The war," Tolstoy answered, "was bound to happen simply because it was bound to happen." All prior history predetermined it. As for leaders, they, Tolstoy said, "are but the labels that serve to give a name to an end and, like labels, they have the least possible connection with the event." The greater the leader, "the more conspicuous the inevitability and the predestination of every act he commits." The leader, said Tolstoy, is "the slave of history."

Determinism takes many forms. Marxism is the determinism of class. Nazism the determinism of race. But the idea of men and women as the slaves of history runs athwart the deepest human instincts. Rigid determinism abolishes the idea of human freedom—

the assumption of free choice that underlies every move we make, every word we speak, every thought we think. It abolishes the idea of human responsibility, since it is manifestly unfair to reward or punish people for actions that are by definition beyond their control. No one can live consistently by any deterministic creed. The Marxist states prove this themselves by their extreme susceptibility to the cult of leadership.

More than that, history refutes the idea that individuals make no difference. In December 1931 a British politician crossing Park Avenue in New York City between 76th and 77th Streets around 10:30 P.M. looked in the wrong direction and was knocked down by an automobile—a moment, he later recalled, of a man aghast, a world aglare: "I do not understand why I was not broken like an eggshell or squashed like a gooseberry." Fourteen months later an American politician, sitting in an open car in Miami, Florida, was fired on by an assassin; the man beside him was hit. Those who believe that individuals make no difference to history might well ponder whether the next two decades would have been the same had Mario Constasino's car killed Winston Churchill in 1931 and Giuseppe Zangara's bullet killed Franklin Roosevelt in 1933. Suppose, in addition, that Adolf Hitler had been killed in the street fighting during the Munich *Putsch* of 1923 and that Lenin had died of typhus during World War I. What would the 20th century be like now?

For better or for worse, individuals do make a difference. "The notion that a people can run itself and its affairs anonymously," wrote the philosopher William James, "is now well known to be the silliest of absurdities. Mankind does nothing save through initiatives on the part of inventors, great or small, and imitation by the rest of us—these are the sole factors in human progress. Individuals of genius show the way, and set the patterns, which common people then adopt and follow."

Leadership, James suggests, means leadership in thought as well as in action. In the long run, leaders in thought may well make the greater difference to the world. But, as Woodrow Wilson once said, "Those only are leaders of men, in the general eye, who lead in action. . . . It is at their hands that new thought gets its translation into the crude language of deeds." Leaders in thought often invent in solitude and obscurity, leaving to later generations the tasks of imitation. Leaders in action—the leaders portrayed in this series—have to be effective in their own time.

And they cannot be effective by themselves. They must act in response to the rhythms of their age. Their genius must be adapted, in a phrase of William James's, "to the receptivities of the moment." Leaders are useless without followers. "There goes the mob," said the French politician hearing a clamor in the streets. "I am their leader. I must follow them." Great leaders turn the inchoate emotions of the mob to purposes of their own. They seize on the opportunities of their time, the hopes, fears, frustrations, crises, potentialities. They succeed when events have prepared the way for them, when the community is awaiting to be aroused, when they can provide the clarifying and organizing ideas. Leadership ignites the circuit between the individual and the mass and thereby alters history.

It may alter history for better or for worse. Leaders have been responsible for the most extravagant follies and most monstrous crimes that have beset suffering humanity. They have also been vital in such gains as humanity has made in individual freedom, religious and racial tolerance, social justice and respect for human rights.

There is no sure way to tell in advance who is going to lead for good and who for evil. But a glance at the gallery of men and women in *World Leaders—Past and Present* suggests some useful tests.

One test is this: do leaders lead by force or by persuasion? By command or by consent? Through most of history leadership was exercised by the divine right of authority. The duty of followers was to defer and to obey. "Theirs not to reason why,/ Theirs but to do and die." On occasion, as with the so-called "enlightened despots" of the 18th century in Europe, absolutist leadership was animated by humane purposes. More often, absolutism nourished the passion for domination, land, gold and conquest and resulted in tyranny.

The great revolution of modern times has been the revolution of equality. The idea that all people should be equal in their legal condition has undermined the old structure of authority, hierarchy and deference. The revolution of equality has had two contrary effects on the nature of leadership. For equality, as Alexis de Tocqueville pointed out in his great study *Democracy in America*, might mean equality in servitude as well as equality in freedom.

"I know of only two methods of establishing equality in the political world," Tocqueville wrote. "Rights must be given to every citizen, or none at all to anyone . . . save one, who is the master of all." There was no middle ground "between the sovereignty of all and the absolute power of one man." In his astonishing prediction of 20th-century totalitarian dictatorship, Tocqueville explained how the revolution of equality could lead to the *"Führerprinzip"* and more terrible absolutism than the world had ever known.

But when rights are given to every citizen and the sovereignty of all is established, the problem of leadership takes a new form, becomes more exacting than ever before. It is easy to issue commands and enforce them by the rope and the stake, the concentration camp and the *gulag.* It is much harder to use argument and achievement to overcome opposition and win consent. The Founding Fathers of the United States understood the difficulty. They believed that history had given them the opportunity to decide, as Alexander Hamilton wrote in the first Federalist Paper, whether men are indeed capable of basing government on "reflection and choice, or whether they are forever destined to depend . . . on accident and force."

Government by reflection and choice called for a new style of leadership and a new quality of followership. It required leaders to be responsive to popular concerns, and it required followers to be active and informed participants in the process. Democracy does not eliminate emotion from politics; sometimes it fosters demagoguery; but it is confident that, as the greatest of democratic leaders put it, you cannot fool all of the people all of the time. It measures leadership by results and retires those who overreach or falter or fail.

It is true that in the long run despots are measured by results too. But they can postpone the day of judgment, sometimes indefinitely, and in the meantime they can do infinite harm. It is also true that democracy is no guarantee of virtue and intelligence in government, for the voice of the people is not necessarily the voice of God. But democracy, by assuring the right of opposition, offers built-in resistance to the evils inherent in absolutism. As the theologian Reinhold Niebuhr summed it up, "Man's capacity for justice makes democracy possible, but man's inclination to injustice makes democracy necessary."

A second test for leadership is the end for which power is sought. When leaders have as their goal the supremacy of a master race or the promotion of totalitarian revolution or the acquisition and exploitation of colonies or the protection of greed and privilege or the preservation of personal power, it is likely that their leadership will do little to advance the cause of humanity. When their goal is the abolition of slavery, the liberation of women, the enlargement of opportunity for the poor and powerless, the extension of equal rights to racial minorities, the defense of the freedoms of expression and opposition, it is likely that their leadership will increase the sum of human liberty and welfare.

Leaders have done great harm to the world. They have also conferred great benefits. You will find both sorts in this series. Even "good" leaders must be regarded with a certain wariness. Leaders are not demigods; they put on their trousers one leg after another just like ordinary mortals. No leader is infallible, and every leader needs to be reminded of this at regular intervals. Irreverence irritates leaders but is their salvation. Unquestioning submission corrupts leaders and demands followers. Making a cult of a leader is always a mistake. Fortunately hero worship generates its own antidote. "Every hero," said Emerson, "becomes a bore at last."

The signal benefit the great leaders confer is to embolden the rest of us to live according to our own best selves, to be active, insistent, and resolute in affirming our own sense of things. For great leaders attest to the reality of human freedom against the supposed inevitabilities of history. And they attest to the wisdom and power that may lie within the most unlikely of us, which is why Abraham Lincoln remains the supreme example of great leadership. A great leader, said Emerson, exhibits new possibilities to all humanity. "We feed on genius. . . . Great men exist that there may be greater men."

Great leaders, in short, justify themselves by emancipating and empowering their followers. So humanity struggles to master its destiny, remembering with Alexis de Tocqueville: "It is true that around every man a fatal circle is traced beyond which he cannot pass; but within the wide verge of that circle he is powerful and free; as it is with man, so with communities."

1

The Mad Aristocrat

France and the powerful kingdom of Prussia stood at the brink of war in July 1870. The cause of the confrontation was Prince Leopold of Hohenzollern-Sigmaringen, a relative of the Prussian king, Wilhelm I. Prince Leopold had just been offered the throne of Spain, and he stood ready to accept — with the encouragement of the Prussian prime minister, Otto von Bismarck.

For Bismarck, this was a crafty stroke of diplomacy. He had outfoxed his chief adversary, Emperor Napoleon III of France, better known as Louis-Napoléon. If Leopold became king of Spain, France would be surrounded by two potentially hostile neighbors — the Spanish to the south, allied with the Prussians to the east. To prevent that, France might go to war, but it would then be branded an aggressor by the rest of Europe, and all of the German states would fight on the side of Prussia. Bismarck calculated that war with France would

I am God's soldier, and where He sends me, there I must go. . . . He shapes my life as He needs it.
—OTTO VON BISMARCK

A portrait of Otto von Bismarck painted in 1836. Wildly mischievous as a youth, Bismarck showed little respect for his teachers or peers; only later did he exhibit the conservative values he had inherited.

achieve his greatest dream — a unified German nation under Prussian domination, which, in turn, he would govern.

Wilhelm, however, had no stomach for fighting. He put pressure on Leopold's father, and on July 12 the prince's candidacy was withdrawn. All Europe breathed a sigh of relief, but Bismarck was outraged. His grand scheme, he protested, had been destroyed by Wilhelm's weak-willed capitulation to French threats.

Then a French blunder gave Bismarck the opportunity he wanted. Wilhelm was staying at the resort town of Ems, and on July 13 he ventured out for a morning stroll. He happened to meet the French ambassador, Count Vincente Benedetti, who made a startling request. The ambassador insisted that Leopold's withdrawal was not enough. The French government wanted Wilhelm to pledge that he would never again try to place the prince on the throne of Spain.

Prussian King Wilhelm I, Bismarck's beloved monarch. Bismarck once said, "I feel I am serving God when I serve the king," and ultimately Bismarck's tombstone read, "A true German servant of Kaiser Wilhelm I."

Wilhelm was deeply offended. Diplomatic etiquette does not permit ambassadors to demand promises from kings in full public view. Wilhelm politely but firmly refused to make such a commitment. When Benedetti persisted, the king coolly replied that he had nothing more to say, tipped his hat, and walked away.

One of Wilhelm's aides wrote a report of the encounter and telegraphed it to Bismarck. When the prime minister received the dispatch, he immediately saw his chance. The telegram contained nothing that was shocking or explosive until Bismarck took his pencil to it. By merely cutting out a few passages, he made it appear that Wilhelm had insulted the French ambassador and broken off negotiations. Bismarck then released the edited "Ems telegram" to the press and waited for the blowup.

Denouncing the Ems incident as a deliberate "slap in the face," an affront to its honor, the French government walked blindly into the trap. On July 19 France gave Bismarck what he wanted — a declaration of war. By January the French army had been smashed by the Prussians, and King Wilhelm was proclaimed emperor, or *Kaiser*, of a united Germany.

Otto von Bismarck has become recognized as a legendary master of *Realpolitik* — the politics of realism, practical politics. The Ems telegram affair reveals something remarkable about his character as well as his political methods. For Bismarck, politics was a matter of sheer power. Because he held such harsh views, it is commonly thought that he cared nothing for idealism, morality, honesty, or human rights. Using both skillful diplomacy and ruthless military force, he made Germany the strongest nation in 19th-century Europe. In Bismarck's defense, the British historian A. J. P. Taylor claims that Bismarck "did not lack principles. . . . They were principles founded in distrust of human nature."

Bismarck was born on April 1, 1815. At the time, Germany was not a single unified state but a patchwork of 35 independent monarchies and 4 free

The French ambassador Count Vincente Benedetti insisted to Wilhelm in July 1870 that he promise to not attempt to make Prince Leopold of Hohenzollern-Sigmaringen (a relative of Wilhelm's) king of Spain. Bismarck's carefully edited account of the exchange, the famous Ems telegram, made war between France and Prussia inevitable.

cities, all loosely grouped in the German Confederation, which in turn was dominated by the sprawling Austrian Empire. After Austria, the largest German state was Prussia, which extended over much of northern Germany and included the Rhineland and what are now East Germany and western Poland.

The Prussian army and government bureaucracy were led by landowning nobles, or *Junkers*. Most of them were not especially worldly or well educated. They were content to farm their country estates and serve the Prussian royal family — the house of Hohenzollern.

The Bismarcks lived in the small town of Schönhausen in Brandenburg, a province within Prussia, and their family was even older than the ruling Hohenzollerns. Ferdinand von Bismarck-Schönhausen, Otto's father, was a slow-witted man, neither a dedicated soldier nor a particularly good farmer. His wife, Wilhelmine, was a more formidable person. Her father, Ludwig Mencken, was one of the most renowned civil servants of the day and a close adviser to three Prussian kings, including Friedrich Wilhelm III. Wilhelmine was something of an intellectual and was fascinated by the fashionable 19th-century trends of spiritualism, hypnotism, and religious mysticism. Ideas like democracy, greater political freedom, and the involvement of workers and peasants in how they were governed were being discussed, and Bismarck's mother took an interest in these as well.

Wilhelmine was intensely concerned about her sons' futures. (Bismarck had a brother, Bernhard, and a sister, Malwine.) She hoped, she said, that they would someday "penetrate far deeper into the world of ideas than has been possible for me, a mere woman." Accordingly, the six-year-old Bismarck was sent to Berlin to study at the Plamann Institute. It was a respected boarding school, and Wilhelmine was also pleased to have a reason to visit the city. He attended other schools there, and in 1830 he became a student at the *Graue Kloster Gymnasium*. But the young Bismarck sorely missed the family estate. For the rest of his life, he hated Berlin. He grew to dislike intellectuals, although he admired the Romantic poet George Gordon, Lord Byron, the English playwright William Shakespeare, and Friedrich von Schiller, the German playwright. The adventure novels of Scottish writer Sir Walter Scott held a certain appeal for him as well. He also tried to be a member of the *Burschenschaften*, or student unions. These organizations were devoted to the revolutionary and reformist ideals that sprang up in Prussia during the 1813 War of Liberation against the French conqueror and emperor Napoleon Bonaparte. The groups were not to his liking. Their liberal views reflected those of the new middle class, not those of the old Prussian nobility into which he had been born. Perhaps all that he learned from these students was to smoke cigars, a rare habit among Prussians. As a statesman Bismarck would try to preserve those traditions he regarded as being of the Junker class. He became a champion of strict conservative values — specifically respect for power and obedience to authority.

As a young man, however, Bismarck seemed to have no respect for authority. From 1832 until 1833 he was enrolled at the University of Göttingen in the German kingdom of Hannover, where he devoted himself to drinking, carousing, chasing young women, and wearing dandyish clothes. One night a flying bottle shattered a window at a local tavern, and Bismarck was summoned to the university rector's office the following morning. The rector demanded that the young gentleman kindly explain how this had happened.

"Presumably a bottle flew out of the window . . . of its own volition!" Bismarck replied.

"Indeed. Would you care to be more explicit?"

Bismarck quietly took a paperweight from the rector's desk and cupped it menacingly in his hand, as if he were preparing to pitch it through the window. "Get the idea?" he snarled, and strode out of the office.

The rowdy student was already learning how he would deal with his adversaries — with force or threats of force. He fought 25 duels at Göttingen and won nearly all of them. Bismarck could never bear to lose a fight. Once he was injured in a fencing match, and for years he stubbornly insisted that his opponent had struck a foul blow.

Bismarck lasted less than a year at Göttingen. He transferred to the University of Berlin, where he barely managed to pass his examinations. His mother had important connections at court, however, and her son began to meet members of the Prussian royal family. Those connections helped him win an attractive civil service post at Aachen (Aix-la-Chapelle), a spa in the Rhineland.

Bismarck was not destined for life as a civil servant. He disliked routine paperwork, and he could not follow orders. Neglecting his duties, he gambled away large sums of money and enjoyed the company of wealthy tourists. For a while he was infatuated with an English girl, the niece of the duchess of Cleveland. Then, for several months, he pursued another English girl as far as Switzerland — until he remembered that he had a job back in Aachen. He wrote an apology to his superiors but insisted that he could not return to his post until he had cleared up this bit of private business. When asked to explain his absence, Bismarck bluntly replied that he "by no means intended to give the government an account of his personal relations."

Bismarck was suspended from his job, but his mother's connections enabled him to obtain another civil service position, at Potsdam, which he left after three months. His defection meant that he was no longer able to postpone his mandatory military service. Headstrong and willful, unable to defer to authority, he was desperately eager to avoid the army, but he completed his military obligation.

In 1839 Bismarck left the Prussian army and officially resigned from the civil service. "I have never been able to put up with superiors," he once explained. "The Prussian official is like a member of an orchestra [who must follow the score]. But *I* want to play only the music I like, or none at all." In fact, he wanted to be the conductor. He wanted to command, to be admired, to win fame, but now, at age 24, Bismarck had no career at all.

He tried his hand at running one of his family's estates, in Kniephof, near the city of Stettin, in north-central Germany. He soon found the life of the rural gentry lonely and tedious, relieved only by wild practical jokes. On one occasion he let a fox loose in a lady's drawing room and on another awakened a friend by firing a gun through his window. His terrified neighbors called him "the mad Junker." To get away from home, he considered joining the British army in India but decided against it. "I asked myself what harm the Indians had done to me," he explained years later.

Bismarck was lifted out of his rut only by marriage and a religious conversion. Several of his friends were Pietists, members of a highly devout sect of Lutherans. (Lutheranism is a branch of Protes-

> *By now he was 30, bitter, cynical, and neurotic, his gifts running to nothing. New life came unexpectedly with religion, a wife, and a revolution.*
> —A. J. P. TAYLOR
> British historian, on
> Bismarck in 1844

tantism based on the teachings of Martin Luther, the 16-century German religious reformer and leader of the Reformation.) Lutherans formed the overwhelming majority in Prussia. In the southern German states, Catholicism predominated. Bismarck believed in God, but he insisted on holding his own opinions concerning this belief and did not involve himself at all deeply in religious questions. His driving concerns were almost entirely political, focusing on power — his own and that of the German nation he would create. He regarded Roman Catholicism with suspicion, and years later, as German imperial chancellor, he launched a political attack against the German Catholic clergy. Previously, Bismarck had never much cared for religion, but in 1844 he became attracted to a lovely young Pietist, Marie von Thadden, who was soon to marry one of Bismarck's old school friends. Both tried to convert him. That same year he tried — briefly — to work at his old civil service post. On November 11, 1846, Marie died as a result of an epidemic. Bismarck was emotionally shattered by the tragedy.

He then fell in love with Marie's close friend Johanna von Puttkamer. She was neither beautiful nor brilliant, but her suitor appreciated her simple religious devotion and was determined to marry her. Johanna's father, however, would allow her to marry only a devout Christian. Bismarck rose to that challenge. In a dramatic letter to Herr von Puttkamer, he passionately proclaimed his religious faith. The old gentleman was overwhelmed, and in July 1847 the couple was married.

While Bismarck had professed being religious, he was not entirely sincere. It was partly a clever piece of diplomacy designed to win the hand of Johanna. "I think I am entitled to count myself among the adherents of the Christian religion," he once said to his brother, Bernhard. "Though in many doctrines, perhaps in those which they regard as essential, I am far removed from their standpoint, yet a sort of treaty . . . has been silently established between us [God and Bismarck]."

All the same, the mad Junker did benefit from religious teaching. He had seemed not to want to

At the age of 32 Bismarck married Johanna von Putt-kamer, pictured here. Bismarck overcame the major obstacle to their being married — Johanna's father's refusal to allow his daughter to marry a non-Christian — by proclaiming his newfound religious faith.

grow up and had wasted the first 32 years of his life. He always appeared to be bursting with energy but in the past squandered much of it on high living and schoolboy pranks. At last, Christianity gave him the self-discipline he sorely needed. The mischievous young man was transformed into a sober, puritanical, Bible-reading family man.

Now Bismarck found a real purpose in his life, in politics. "I feel I am serving God when I serve the king," he affirmed. He would stop at nothing to achieve his political goals, because he was certain that God was on his side. As one diplomat acidly remarked, "If Bismarck believes in his God, God himself must be a Prussian." Years later, when his policies were succeeding in bringing about a united German empire, Bismarck attributed his own greatness to the "wonderful basis of religion."

2
The Year of Revolution

On January 12, 1848, the people of Sicily revolted against their oppressive king, Ferdinand II. Within a month the rebellion had spread throughout Italy. By February 22 the tide of revolution had reached Paris, where citizens armed themselves and barricaded the streets. Two days later, King Louis-Philippe of France abdicated, and a provisional government was proclaimed. News of the Paris rebellion traveled rapidly to Vienna in Austria and Budapest in Hungary, and the populations rose up in revolt. By March the unrest had reached as far as Berlin, the capital of Prussia.

Thus began one of the greatest revolutionary upheavals in history. Armed citizens in Italy, France, Austria, and Germany demanded national self-government and an end to autocracy (government in which a monarch or leader possesses absolute power). All of the revolutions of 1848 eventually died down or were crushed, but for a time they convulsed half of Europe.

Bismarck stepped into the political spotlight on May 17, 1847, when, as a representative to the United Diet, he verbally attacked current liberal proposals — boldly denouncing the adoption of a constitution and insisting that the king give up none of his authority.

> *Great crises are the very weather for Prussia's growth, if we take advantage of them fearlessly and, perhaps, very recklessly.*
> —OTTO VON BISMARCK

The coronation of King Ferdinand II of the Two Sicilies (southern Italy and Sicily). On January 12, 1848, the people of Sicily revolted against Ferdinand's oppressive regime, igniting a revolutionary fire that spread throughout half of Europe that year.

Europe in the 1840s was still ruled very much as it had been ruled in preceding centuries — by kings, princes, and aristocrats. Now the middle and working classes were demanding freedom and the right to participate in government. The French Revolution of 1789, the forerunner of the radical and reformist concerns that became so important during the 1840s, had infected the continent with the spirit of nationalism and democracy.

Nationalism, the belief that national communities or groups should be independent and self-determining along with a pride in, and loyalty to, one's nation, and democracy, the belief that the individual should have a say in how he is governed, soon became associated with liberalism. A growing movement in Europe at this time, liberalism represented the need for political and economic freedom. Liberals demanded self-determination for the individual and governmental reforms that would encourage personal liberty. During the 1830s liberal students and intellectuals in Germany were drawn to the nationalist Young Germany movement.

In the late 18th and early 19th centuries, nationalism captured the imaginations of many Germans who were influenced by the theories of the philosopher and educator Johann Gottfried von Herder. While Herder maintained that each nationality possessed its own separate and distinguishing folk heritage, he opposed the most extreme form of nationalism: the belief that a particular country is inherently superior to, and should therefore dominate, other nations.

Eighteenth-century German philosopher, educator, and poet Johann Gottfried von Herder developed theories of national and folk culture that influenced German nationalists, many of whom were critical of the Prussian state Bismarck defended.

Prussia's King Friedrich Wilhelm IV stubbornly resisted granting a national constitution and denounced the idea of popular representation in government. He believed in the divine right of kings and dreamed of restoring a rule of landowners based on a medieval model.

Prussian nationalists were dissatisfied with the Hohenzollern monarchy that ruled Prussia. They were displeased with the state officials and military that ran Prussia with indifference toward the people's wishes. Not only would government improve if reformed, they claimed, but the German people would be more secure if the various German states or principalities were unified. Under the weak German Confederation, established in 1815, these states were not truly united. Instead, they tried to protect their own political and territorial interests against their German-speaking neighbors. The smaller states were caught between the two most powerful ones: Prussia and Austria, which were rivals for control of the confederation.

It was thought by many nationalists that Prussia was defeated by Napoleon in 1806 and 1807 because power belonged solely to the king, his officials, and the military. The people had no voice in how they were ruled. Thus they had done little to oppose Napoleon's armies, leaving the task to the government, which had badly managed the war. Liberals believed the autocratic Prussian state was merely an artificial government. It was very likely, they thought, that without a more democratic process it would crumble altogether. The great 18th-century German writer Novalis once stated, "No state had been governed more like a factory than Prussia." Students, intellectuals, artists, journalists, and lawyers passionately proclaimed that people who shared a common language, culture, and history should have a unified state of their own. In an age of powerful new political ideals, King Friedrich Wilhelm IV of Prussia was living in a distant past. He spoke about providing a representative form of government but dreamed of restoring the rule of landowners as it existed in the Middle Ages. He unquestioningly believed in the doctrine of the divine right of kings, that is, that kings had a right to rule by power said to be vested in them by God. Friedrich Wilhelm was a benevolent monarch, basically decent and kind to his subjects but also indecisive and unrealistic. He treated his subjects as if they were children. He genuinely wanted to be a good ruler, but he would never allow them to rule themselves. During the period from 1840 to 1848, known as the *Vormärz*, representatives of the middle classes called on the king for a written constitution and a representative assembly. Such leaders included the Prussian industrialists Gustav Mevissen and David Hansemann, who also was Prussian finance minister. The poorer classes in Prussia were discontented and hungry. The economy had gone into a decline; food shortages had brought about riots called the "potato revolution" in 1847.

Although the famed Prussian philosopher Georg Wilhelm Friedrich Hegel had defended the Prussian state in his writings, after his death some of his followers began to use his ideas to criticize, rather than praise, the government. One of them was Karl Marx, who in the 1840s was editor of an influential radical newspaper. Marx, with his collaborator, Friedrich Engels, developed political and economic theories that stated that capitalism (private ownership of industry) would eventually be overthrown by the workers, or "proletariat," and replaced by socialism. They predicted that ultimately a society without classes would result. French socialist thinkers also made a significant impact on Prussians desiring representational government.

Friedrich Wilhelm's father, King Friedrich Wilhelm III, had made a promise to establish a constitutional government. When Friedrich Wilhelm succeeded his father as king in 1840, many Prussians hoped for representation and a constitution. They were soon proved wrong. The new king was stubbornly against these proposals. He instead chose to create a "United Diet," or *Landtag*. There was no parliament in Prussia, but there were eight provincial assemblies, which were now commanded to send deputies to Berlin. It was not a permanent assembly, meeting only under special circumstances. In the spring of 1847 it met for the first time. The king's address on that occasion made clear that the diet would be mainly for show and would not have a constitution. Friedrich Wilhelm declared, "Never will I permit a piece of paper to come between God in heaven and this land."

Very few of the delegates were supporters of the king. Most were liberals. One of the diet's members was Bismarck, who had been elected as an alternate to replace an elderly representative who had fallen ill. Thus Bismarck stepped into the drama of history — as an understudy — and immediately shocked his audience. On May 17 he took his first plunge into politics by rudely attacking the liberal delegates. He spoke like a rebel but was intensely conservative. He bitterly attacked every liberal proposal. He thought that the king should give up none of his authority. In particular, he abused and misrepresented an honored war veteran who had spoken in favor of a constitution.

The history of all hitherto existing society is the history of class struggles.
—KARL MARX
founder of communism

The diet was appalled. In a country where old soldiers were revered, this impudent young reactionary had taunted a national hero in his very first speech. The chamber resounded with protests. Unable to speak above the din, Bismarck coldly took up a newspaper and pretended to read it. That was a brilliant theatrical stroke, for without saying a word he had displayed his limitless contempt for parliamentary government.

Bismarck did not want to abolish the diet after all. That would have ended his political career. But he stubbornly resisted every reform and defended Friedrich Wilhelm on every point. Bismarck's manner was so insolent, his conservatism so rigid, that even the king disliked him. Friedrich Wilhelm would not deign to thank, or even speak to, his most ardent supporter.

Philosopher and economist Karl Marx. With his collaborator, Friedrich Engels, Marx developed theories that predicted the bankruptcy of capitalism and the inevitable actualization of a society without class distinctions. Such theories appealed to Prussians in favor of representational government.

Prussia trembled in 1848 as the masses demonstrated their demand for a representational government. The palace of the prince of Prussia was declared national property in one such demonstration in Berlin.

Without a constitution the diet refused to approve a railway loan the king had requested, so the king sent the delegates home. The revolution had only just begun. By March 17, 1848, Berlin was convulsed by demonstrations demanding a united constitutional government for all of Germany.

Friedrich Wilhelm seemed to be in a state of confusion. His generals wanted to suppress the rebellion by force, but the king called the diet back into session to draft a constitution. In Berlin, the following day, troops fired into a crowd of citizens who were protesting in front of the royal palace. That incident inflamed the situation beyond control. By evening barricades had been erected all over Berlin. One general told Friedrich Wilhelm that the army would soon have only one option — to lay siege to the city and starve it into capitulation.

The crisis was too much for the weak-willed monarch. Acting on his confused orders, on March 18 the army withdrew to the suburb of Potsdam, leaving the king to the mercy of the revolution. The rebels surrounded the royal palace and commanded Friedrich Wilhelm to pay homage to the citizens who had been killed the previous night. The monarch came out and stood bareheaded before the corpses that lay in the street. Two days later he announced that Prussia would "merge" with a united Germany.

All this time Bismarck had been visiting friends in the country, unaware of the upheaval in Berlin. When the news arrived he raced home to his estate at Schönhausen. There he distributed weapons to loyal peasants. He threatened to shoot a neighbor who had dared to suggest that Bismarck might be overreacting. Having secured Schönhausen against the revolution, he dashed off to rescue the king.

In Potsdam, Bismarck offered to raise an army of peasants to fight the rebels. The generals told him to go home and send food and supplies for their soldiers. Instead, Bismarck disguised himself as a revolutionary and went to Berlin. After unsuccessfully attempting to gain entry to the royal palace in Berlin, Bismarck managed to get a note in to the beleaguered king. Since Friedrich Wilhelm would not fight, Bismarck seriously suggested that the king abdicate in favor of his 16-year-old nephew, Friedrich, who would then serve as a figurehead while actual power rested elsewhere, possibly in the hands of the loyal Bismarck. Such measures had

An 1848 engraving depicts mixed public reaction to a poster calling for the ouster of Prince Klemens von Metternich, chancellor of Austria. Metternich was indeed forced to flee; he took refuge in England and then Belgium, where he stayed until the revolutionary tide subsided.

Behind the barricades in Berlin, young boys cast lead bullets during the 1848 revolution. The forces of liberalism, nationalism, democracy, and modern industrialization all came into play in the Europe of 1848, creating a surge of revolutionary activity.

been taken in Austria against the revolution there, bringing Franz Josef to the Austrian throne. Friedrich's mother, Princess Augusta, wife of the king's brother Wilhelm, would have nothing to do with the scheme, which would force Wilhelm, who was in line to succeed Friedrich Wilhelm, to renounce his claim. An astute woman, Augusta saw that Bismarck was trying to use the royal family to win power for himself, and she became one of his most determined enemies.

Friedrich Wilhelm kept his promise and granted Prussia a parliament. In April 1848 the diet proposed a vote of thanks, but this time Bismarck could not support his king. The monarch, he protested, had betrayed the monarchy. "The past is buried," he said sadly, ". . . the crown itself has cast earth upon its coffin." Then, on the brink of tears, he could say no more. As an ultraconservative, Bismarck could not hope to win election to a truly democratic parliament. In a new liberal Germany, it seemed, he would have no political future. The diet had decided on indirect elections for representatives to a Prussian parliament. At about the same time the independent city of Frankfurt prepared to welcome 800 deputies to the National Assembly, which was to convene to discuss German unification on May 18, 1848. Bismarck was not one of them. The liberals and nationalists in the National Assembly (or Frankfurt Parliament) had their own plan for establishing an independent, united nation of Germany. The most crucial issue was whether the entire Austrian Empire would be a part of the new state. In December the assembly accepted a plan that did not include Austria — the "lesser Germany," or *Kleindeutschland* solution.

Even though the parliament wanted to make the Prussian king the emperor of this proposed German nation, Friedrich Wilhelm rejected the plan. Bismarck, who at first favored the plan, soon sided with the king on this issue. Bismarck believed in Germany's unification, yet felt it would be a mistake under the existing constitution. Bismarck was an

The Prussian army clashes with revolutionaries in Frankfurt, September 1848. Bismarck secured the safety of his own estate at Schönhausen by arming loyal peasants and enlisting them as protectors.

As 1848 came to an end so did the revolutionary fervor that had shaken Europe. In France, Louis-Napoléon, pictured here, became president (later he would name himself Emperor Napoleon III). In Prussia Friedrich Wilhelm dissolved the parliament, proclaiming his own constitution.

impatient and complicated man. While his principles seemed conservative, his methods were flamboyant — even radical. He wanted to change events. He viewed parliamentary government with contempt, yet it was as a delegate in the United Diet, as the monarchy's defender, that his career actually began. He would not remain steadily a conservative. Whatever position best served his own will was the one he would choose. His opportunities lay, as he said, with the "current of the times."

Friedrich Wilhelm invited the young firebrand Bismarck to dinner and tried to explain his actions to him. A monarch could not massacre his own people, the king said. Friedrich Wilhelm's wife, Queen Elizabeth, said that the king at the height of the revolution had been sick with worry, unable to sleep for days. Bismarck was not impressed. "A king *must* be able to sleep," he said. (In his memoirs, however, Bismarck claimed not to have made this statement.) He could never quite forgive Friedrich Wilhelm for refusing to stand up to what the Junker considered a mob.

By the end of the year, however, the revolution had burned itself out. In Austria the imperial army regrouped and shelled the rebels in Vienna into submission. In France Louis-Napoléon, the nephew of Napoleon Bonaparte, was elected president, and four years later he would proclaim himself emperor, becoming Napoleon III. In Prussia Friedrich Wilhelm felt strong enough to dissolve the Prussian parliament in November 1848. He proclaimed his own constitution, under which he retained nearly all his political power. Prussia would still have a parliament, but because it was elected on a much less democratic basis, the outspoken and arrogant Bismarck was elected to the second chamber in 1849.

Friedrich Wilhelm also sent the Prussian army to stamp out revolts throughout Germany, particularly those in Frankfurt, Saxony, Bavaria, and Baden, where they had first broken out. The German princes were only too glad to receive help from the Prussian army. However, they were now dependent on Prussian military force. Friedrich Wilhelm realized that he was in a strong position to create a new German federation under Prussian domination. He went so far as to convene a parliament, which met at Erfurt (the Erfurt Union) in April 1850 to discuss a plan for a union of German states under Prussian control.

The Austrians, however, were eager to regain control over the German states — by force if necessary. The two nations mobilized their armies and very nearly went to war, but Prussia was still too weak to challenge Austria. Friedrich Wilhelm was forced to sign the humiliating Treaty of Olmütz, which ended the Erfurt Union and restored the old Austrian-dominated German Confederation. The cruel, often deceptive Austrian foreign minister, Prince Felix Schwarzenberg, gloated over this victory.

One member of the Erfurt Union welcomed this defeat for Prussia — none other than Bismarck. War with Austria would have only "made us shoot and

The great questions of the day will be decided not by speeches and majority votes — that was the great mistake of 1848 and 1849 — but by blood and iron.
—OTTO VON BISMARCK

On May 18, 1848, the German National Assembly met in Frankfurt to discuss plans for unifying Germany. Bismarck continued to be the staunch conservative, defending the monarchy and denouncing the constitution, and was not one of the 800 elected deputies.

kill our German fellow countrymen," he argued. "It is unworthy of a great state to fight for something which does not affect its own interest. Show me, gentlemen, an objective worth a war, and I will go along with you. It is easy enough for a statesman to ride the popular wave from the comfort of his own fireside, making thunderous speeches from the rostrum, letting the public sound the trumpets of war, and leaving it to the musketeer, bleeding out his life's blood in the snowy wastes, to settle whether policies end in glory or failure. Nothing is simpler — but woe to any statesman who, at such a time, fails to find a cause of war which will stand up to scrutiny once the fighting is over."

Bismarck was quite willing to send thousands of soldiers to die so long as they were fighting for "an objective worth a war." In 1850 he was convinced that the cause of German unity was not worth a war with Austria. German nationalism was still a revolutionary idea, and a Germany unified by parliament would have been much too democratic to suit Bismarck. If he could unite Germany on his own terms, become the conductor of the German orchestra, and impose Prussian conservatism on the rest of the nation, those goals — to Bismarck — would be worth three cold-blooded wars.

3

An Unlikely Diplomat

In 1851 Bismarck was chosen to be Prussia's ambassador to the *Bundestag*, or the Federal Diet, the governing body of the revived German Confederation. He could not have been more pleased. "Beyond my wildest expectations or desires comes this sudden appointment to what is at this moment the most important post in our diplomatic service," he told his wife. After 1852 he would never again seek a parliamentary seat.

Friedrich Wilhelm entertained serious misgivings about his new ambassador, who had absolutely no diplomatic experience. Still, Bismarck was clearly a man of great ability, someone who knew how to stand up to his enemies. True, he was a troublesome individual, but perhaps, given a responsible job, he would learn to behave himself.

Bismarck learned a great deal about politics at the Bundestag, which met in the independent city of Frankfurt. For the first time he associated with

> *Politics is less a science than an art. It is a subject that cannot be taught, one has to have the gift.*
> —OTTO VON BISMARCK

Otto von Bismarck in 1859. Though relatively inexperienced in affairs of state, Bismarck was chosen as Prussia's representative to the Federal Diet in 1851 despite Friedrich Wilhelm's serious misgivings.

THE BETTMANN ARCHIVE

Austrian statesman Prince Klemens von Metternich was a dominant figure in European diplomacy prior to the 1848 revolution. "The Coachman of Europe" stood for political order above all else; he despised the revolution, calling it "a sickness of the times."

Germans from outside Prussia. He also struck up a friendship with the elderly Austrian statesman Prince Klemens von Metternich. The defeat of the "lesser Germany" plan for unification was a great blow to liberals and to parliamentary government. It also restored to Austria much of its power in German affairs.

As the foreign minister and chancellor of Austria, Metternich had dominated European diplomacy until the 1848 revolution, when he was driven into exile. He had based his foreign policy on legitimacy — the principle that each king had an unquestionable right to his kingdom, as if the kingdom were his personal property. No one, not even another king, could arbitrarily deprive him of that property.

Bismarck cared nothing for legitimacy. He was increasingly determined to impose his will on Germany, and he was prepared to fight any nation that stood in his way, including Austria. "I don't recognize any right in foreign policy," he once growled. "The only healthy foundation for a great state is egoism, not romanticism." To the civilized world of European diplomacy, Bismarck would bring the new ruthlessness of realpolitik.

At the Bundestag, the haughty chairman from Austria, Count Leo von Thun-Hohenstein, refused to treat the Prussians as equals. In retaliation Bismarck vowed to fight the count at every turn: "When Austria hitches a horse in front, we hitch one behind." By tradition only Count Thun could smoke at the Bundestag — so Bismarck defiantly lit up a cigar. When the count attended sessions in shirtsleeves, so did Bismarck. If Thun kept the Prussian delegate waiting for a meeting, Bismarck simply turned around and left.

"The Austrians invariably cheat at cards and always will," he sneered. "I do not see how we can expect ever to make an honest alliance with them." A short time ago Bismarck had urged peace with Austria. Now he told his superiors that they could win more respect from Austria if they would ally themselves with Louis-Napoléon of France.

Although he was only a junior diplomat, Bismarck was already presuming to guide Prussian foreign policy. He made constant trips between Frankfurt and Berlin to argue his views. His proposals were nothing short of revolutionary. Echoing the liberals he had opposed in 1850, he wanted to abandon Prussia's traditional ally and join forces with her traditional enemy. His superiors in Berlin were shocked. They regarded Emperor Louis-Napoléon as a threat to Prussia and to the peace of Europe, just as his uncle Napoleon Bonaparte, who had conquered much of the continent, had been. Bismarck, however, realized that this younger Napoleon was much too timid to be a world conqueror. After meeting Louis-Napoléon in Paris in 1855, he told the Prussian king that the French emperor was "not so clever as the world esteems him." As for the Austrian alliance, Bismarck had no sentimental attachments to that. "I am Prussian," he once wrote. "I would with equal satisfaction see our troops fire on French, Russian, English, or Austrian troops" in the interests of Prussia.

In 1856 Bismarck saw an opportunity to bring Austria to heel. The Crimean War (1853-56) was still raging in the Black Sea region, with Russia, with

> *Politics is the art of the next best.*
> —OTTO VON BISMARCK

which Prussia had been allied in the past, battling France, Britain, and Turkey. Austria was threatening to join the anti-Russian alliance. According to treaty obligations, Prussia could send an army only to guard the Russian frontier. Bismarck told Friedrich Wilhelm that Prussia should indeed mobilize her troops — but they should stand ready to attack *either* Austria or Russia. "With 200,000 men," said Bismarck, "Your Majesty would at one stroke become the master of the entire European situation, dictate the peace and secure for Prussia a worthy position in Germany." The upright king refused to double-cross his ally. "A man of Napoléon's sort might commit such acts of violence," he sniffed, "but not I."

While the king favored an alliance with Austria, Bismarck feared that France and Russia would eventually form an alliance. In October 1857 Friedrich Wilhelm was disabled by a stroke. He still had four more years to live, but his brother Wilhelm would govern as prince regent after September 1858. The new ruler and his wife, Augusta, had only contempt for Bismarck's anti-Austrian scheming — "the politics of a schoolboy," Wilhelm sneered. At the Bundestag, in Frankfurt, Bismarck continued to conduct his own reckless foreign policy. He regarded the pro-Austrian Prussian foreign minister, Otto von Manteuffel, with contempt. Bismarck, meanwhile, was scheming to establish an alliance between Prussia, France, and Russia. Then, early in 1859, he was stunned to learn that he was being recalled from Frankfurt and appointed ambassador to Russia.

Seemingly exiled to the cold northern capital of St. Petersburg (now Leningrad), he felt miserable and humiliated. That summer he fell gravely ill. He suffered pains in the left leg, grossly complicated by a gluttonous diet, the subarctic Russian climate, and the ministrations of an incompetent doctor. For a time it appeared that the leg would have to be amputated, but Bismarck dragged himself home to Berlin and somehow managed to recover. In October he started back to St. Petersburg, but after too

Red reactionary, smells of blood, only to be used when the bayonet rules. . . .
—FRIEDRICH WILHELM IV
king of Prussia,
on Bismarck

A painting entitled *Relief of the Light Brigade,* depicting the 1854 Crimean War battle of Balaclava. Bismarck advised Friedrich Wilhelm to ignore alliances and prepare to enter the war as either Russia's ally or enemy — a suggestion the king found revolting.

much horseback riding and too many of his enormous meals, he contracted pneumonia. The disease nearly killed him. In March 1861 he was cheered by a rumor that Wilhelm might name him prime minister. The prince regent had become King Wilhelm I after Friedrich Wilhelm's death in January. But the ambassador was terribly disappointed when the promotion did not materialize.

The letters of Kurd von Schlözer, an official at the Prussian embassy at St. Petersburg, provide a remarkable insight into Bismarck's character at this time. "My new chief," he noted in April 1859, "is a man with no consideration for others, a man of power who dreams of dramatic gestures, who is anxious to shine, who knows everything without having seen it and affects omniscience although there is much that he does not know." Irascible and uncooperative, Bismarck treated experienced diplomats like office boys. Even during the 1870s, when his power was at its height, he required complete obedience from his staff. "This perpetual harassment by an unscrupulous, neurotic chief who thinks all other men are weaklings, who veils his own plans in darkness . . . who trusts nobody in the world — none of this is very pleasant," complained Schlözer. Bismarck, he observed, "is the wholly political man. His whole being is a ferment of impulses and desires to be expressed, manipulated, shaped. He is determined to command the political arena, . . . but he does not yet know how."

Ignored by his superiors in Berlin, Bismarck did practically no work. He slept until 11:00 A.M. and then spent the rest of the day raging against Austria. Schlözer saw that his chief had great talents but no outlet for his energies. Despite his abilities it seemed that Bismarck — in his own words — had been placed in "cold storage."

For Bismarck, a thaw had begun with new developments in Prussia. General Albrecht von Roon, Prussia's war minister and a close ally of Bismarck, had been working with King Wilhelm on military reorganization. Since 1860 Roon had been planning to reduce the people's militia, the *Landwehr*, and increase compulsory service in the regular

army. Prussia's armed forces would then become less democratic and more firmly under the control of aristocratic officers. This move would strengthen Prussia's autocratic government. At first it seemed the lower house of the Prussian parliament, the *Landtag*, would support Roon's proposal. When the Landtag voted down this plan, Roon proceeded illegally to add new regiments to the army. In November 1861 the liberal Progressive party (the *Deutsche Fortschrittspartei*), opposed to Roon, won impressive gains in the parliamentary election. The minister of war badly wanted his friend Bismarck to be named prime minister. In January King Wilhelm

General Albrecht von Roon, Prussia's minister of war, proposed reforms in an effort to strengthen the autocratic government, specifically through military reorganization. When the parliament rejected his proposals, Roon instituted his policies illegally. Bismarck became Roon's close friend and ally.

Prince Nikolai Orlov, the Russian ambassador to Brussels. In 1861 Bismarck took a vacation in Biarritz, a resort town in southwest France. There he joined Prince Orlov and the prince's wife, Katharina, with whom he became infatuated.

reluctantly agreed to a contingency plan for a military takeover. Fifty thousand soldiers and 100 guns stood ready to disband parliament at bayonet-point and destroy the constitution.

Wilhelm firmly believed in his divine right to rule. Nevertheless, he tried to be tolerant toward parliament and ease repressive policies. He had hoped to help liberals institute reforms, but he expected no interference when he wished to exercise his power as king. Roon realized that there was only one man who could stop the liberals' defiance of the king on the military issue without plunging Prussia into civil war.

Bismarck was called back to Berlin by Roon as early as June 1861. On that occasion he urged Wilhelm to swallow up the smaller German kingdoms by creating an all-German parliament. "I am loyal to my own prince," Bismarck affirmed, " . . . but as for the others I don't feel in one drop of my blood the slightest obligation to lift a finger for them." Wilhelm, who was deeply committed to the principle of legitimacy, repudiated this advice and sent Bismarck back to St. Petersburg. In March 1862 he was recalled to Berlin once again. Although Wilhelm offered to make him prime minister, he still hesitated to entrust Bismarck with control over Prussia's foreign policy. Bismarck would settle for nothing less, and he was prepared to wait. The king would have to learn that he could not rule without Bismarck.

This the king was not yet prepared to do, and in May he appointed Bismarck ambassador to France. That summer Bismarck vacationed at the French resort of Biarritz. There he met an old friend — Prince Nikolai Orlov, the Russian ambassador to Brussels. As he waited for word from Berlin, his career hanging in the balance, Bismarck enjoyed a brief rest from politics. Very soon he fell in love with the prince's very charming and beautiful wife, Katharina.

Bismarck was now 47; Katharina was 22; together they enjoyed music, went picnicking, swimming, and mountain climbing. For the last time in his life, Bismarck felt young and untroubled. "Invisible to all the world, hidden in a steep ravine cut back from the cliffs, I gaze out between two rocks on which the heather blooms at the sea, green and white in the sunshine and the spray," he wrote Johanna. "At my side is the most charming woman, whom you will love very much when you get to know her . . . amusing, intelligent, and kind, pretty, and young."

Neither Johanna nor Prince Orlov seemed to be angered by the dalliance. "Were I at all inclined to

My ambassadors must march in line like soldiers!
—OTTO VON BISMARCK

jealousy and envy I should be tyrannized to the depths now by these passions," Johanna wrote a friend. "But my soul has no room for them and I rejoice quite enormously that my beloved husband has found this charming woman. But for her he would never have found peace for so long in one place or become so well as he boasts of being in every letter." Were it not for Johanna — a tolerant, steady, immensely accommodating woman — Bismarck might never have found a safe harbor from the storms of politics.

On September 12 Bismarck finally wrote to Roon, demanding to know whether or not he would be appointed prime minister. Finally, on September 14, he said farewell to the Orlovs and set out for Paris.

Meanwhile, the power struggle in Berlin was coming to a climax. Wilhelm had lost patience with the Landtag. He did not want to limit the army's size or yield his control of it. Funding for Roon's army was approved by the parliament, which made clear that it would not do so again if it had no say in how the army was run. The king now threatened to abdicate. Roon had to play his last and strongest card. On September 16 Bismarck was sent a telegram summoning him back to Berlin. For 24 hours there was no reply. (Bismarck happened to be out for the day and had not received the message.) Roon, growing desperate, sent a second wire on September 17: "Delay is dangerous. Hurry!"

Three days later Bismarck arrived in Berlin. On September 22 he saw the king and was presented with two documents: a decree of abdication, needing only Wilhelm's signature, and a lengthy memorandum outlining the foreign policy that the king expected his prime minister to follow. In 1859, while still prince regent, Wilhelm had thought that appointing Bismarck as a minister would be "the last straw" and that he would "turn everything upside down." Bismarck now assured Wilhelm that he could handle the parliament and make certain the monarch reigned supreme. He accepted the memorandum, which he had no intention of obeying.

When he left the king's presence, he had been designated prime minister. Within days, he would also be named foreign minister. When Bismarck had become ambassador to France, the Austrian foreign minister, Count Johann Rechberg, commented, "If there is a change of ministry in Prussia, it will be Bismarck's turn and he is capable of pulling off his coat and fighting on the barricades." For the next 27 years he would be the most powerful man in Germany.

4

Blood and Iron

On September 30, 1862, Bismarck appeared before the Prussian parliament to announce his political program. Nervous, speaking in a somewhat shrill voice, he told the delegates that Prussia could not become a great power within her present borders. She needed more territory and therefore required a larger army. "The great questions of the day will be decided not by speeches and majority votes — that was the great mistake of 1848 and 1849," he said, "but by blood and iron."

Nearly every member of the parliament wanted to see a more powerful Prussia, freed from Austrian domination, perhaps part of a unified German empire. On one point Bismarck was right — such an expansionist policy would sooner or later mean war with Austria.

But the parliamentarians were shocked by Bismarck's bluntness. After only a few days in office, he was threatening war. The liberals protested furiously, and even Roon warned Bismarck not to make any more rash speeches. Wilhelm, who was

> *Nothing should be left to an invaded people except their eyes for weeping.*
> —OTTO VON BISMARCK

An 1871 cartoon satirizing Prussian-Austrian relations. From the outset of his term as prime minister Bismarck espoused expansionist policies that he knew would inevitably lead to war with Austria. He shocked the Prussian parliamentarians with his "blood and iron" philosophy.

The crown prince of Prussia, Friedrich Wilhelm (later Emperor Friedrich III), and his wife, Victoria, aligned themselves with the liberal parliamentarians, who sought to limit the power of the Prussian king. Bismarck had only scorn for the idea of a constitutional monarchy.

visiting with his family in the resort town of Baden-Baden, wondered whether he had been wrong to entrust his government to such a reckless politician. Determined to call his new chief minister to account, the king boarded a train for Berlin.

Bismarck realized that he could only save his political career by speaking to Wilhelm alone. On October 4 he intercepted the king at a railroad junction outside of Berlin. He found Wilhelm in a sullen and irritable mood. The king was convinced that Bismarck's high-handedness would lead to revolution. "Under my windows they will cut off your head and soon afterwards mine," the king said.

"And after that, sire?" asked Bismarck.

"After that we shall be dead."

"Yes," Bismarck exclaimed. "After that we shall be dead, but we all have to die sooner or later, and what better way than that? I myself fighting for the cause of my king and Your Majesty . . . sealing your royal prerogative by the Grace of God with your own blood, whether on the scaffold or on the battlefield." It was a brilliant piece of acting. Bismarck knew exactly how to manipulate the romantic monarch. Overwhelmed by this sudden flood of oratory, Wilhelm gave his prime minister his full political support.

With that backing, Bismarck was prepared to confront the parliamentary liberals. They, too, had powerful friends, particularly the king's son, Crown Prince Friedrich Wilhelm (later Emperor Friedrich III), and his wife, Victoria, who was the daughter of Great Britain's Queen Victoria. The crown prince, the crown princess, and the liberals wanted Prussia to become a constitutional monarchy like Britain. The powers of the king would be limited, and the prime minister would represent the majority party in parliament, not the monarch.

Bismarck scornfully replied that Prussia was not Great Britain. He was answerable only to his king, not to the parliament, and any criticism of the king's minister was, he claimed, an attack on the monarchy itself. He responded to his critics by dismissing liberal civil servants and replacing them with loyal, but mediocre, conservatives, and he also corrupted the independence of the Prussian judiciary. Political reliability, not experience, became the criterion for promoting judges.

Like all mediocrities, he likes copying. Fit for stamping letters.
—OTTO VON BISMARCK on Crown Prince Friedrich

Bismarck in 1863. When Bismarck lost a parliamentary vote in May of that year, he dissolved the parliament and censored the press in retaliation. Historian Henry Grosshans wrote of Bismarck, "He had contempt for most of mankind, and once his animosity was aroused he was vindictive and petty."

These measures only stiffened the political opposition to Bismarck. In May 1863 he lost one parliamentary vote by the extreme margin of 295 to 5. In retaliation he dissolved the parliament and persuaded the reluctant king to decree strict press censorship.

"That wretched Bismarck will not stop his mad career until he has plunged his king into ruin and his country into the most dangerous difficulties," protested Princess Victoria. Crown Prince Friedrich publicly denounced the censorship decree, arousing a storm of controversy. One general seriously urged the king to court-martial and jail his son, the prince, for insubordination. Bismarck, however, knew better than to make Friedrich into a martyr for the opposition. He convinced Wilhelm that a simple reprimand would be enough to put the prince in his place.

Meanwhile, Bismarck was pressing forward his policy of Prussian expansion. In that struggle he had an invincible ally — the Industrial Revolution. The small principalities of Germany were relics from

The iron foundry at Lendersdorf, Germany. Prussian industrialists saw expansion as a way of securing rich new sources of raw materials as well as a broader national market for a huge variety of manufactured goods.

Austrian Emperor Franz Josef invited all the ruling German princes to Frankfurt in August 1863. Recognizing the congress as an attempt to strengthen Austrian influence in the German Confederation, Bismarck badgered King Wilhelm until he agreed to decline the invitation.

the Middle Ages. Undeveloped industrially, they did not belong to an era of railroads and factories. By 1860 Germany had overtaken France in coal production and railway mileage. As an industrial power Prussia was far ahead of Austria and the other German states. In 1864 Bismarck himself went to Essen to inspect the huge Krupp ironworks, which were supplying modern weaponry to Wilhelm's army. The cause of German unity found support in a growing class of industrialists, who wanted a large national market for their products. In 1818 Prussia had done away with trade barriers within its own territory. It established the *Zollverein*, or customs union. Southern German states formed their own such union but were later merged into the Prussian one. By 1834, 17 German states were members of the Zollverein, which provided these states with a common market without tariff restrictions. This customs union was a giant step in the direction of political unity. It also gave Prussia enormous financial leverage.

Almost immediately after taking office, Bismarck served notice on the Austrians that Prussia meant to dominate northern Germany, by force if necessary. If Austria cooperated, then Bismarck would be happy to support her elsewhere in Europe. The Austrian foreign minister was unimpressed by this crude bullying and blackmail. He dismissed his Prussian counterpart as a political amateur.

In January 1863 Bismarck was unable to reach an agreement with the liberal parliament. He told its members that if its two chambers could not pass the budget, the king would approve it himself. The king, not the parliament, would make decisions concerning taxes and finance.

A crisis in Poland soon allowed Bismarck to remove one potential enemy from the diplomatic chessboard. At this time Poland was divided between Russia, Prussia, and Austria. In February 1863 the Russian Poles rose up in revolt. A Prussian envoy, Count Albert von Alvensleben-Erxleben, was sent to pledge Prussian support for Russian suppression of the rebels. Bismarck did not want the revolution to spread to Prussia, so he promised to extradite to Russia any Polish rebels who fled across the border.

The Russians brutally crushed the revolt and were condemned by the governments of France, Britain, and Austria. Bismarck also was denounced throughout Europe for helping subdue the Poles. Afterwards it was evident Bismarck had taken a big risk in punishing the Poles, whom he hated. France had considered retaliating against Prussia, while the Russians had been insulted by the Prussians' involvement. Bismarck had feared that Prussian expansion might be opposed by a French-Austrian-Russian coalition, but his actions had earned Prussia the active hostility of both France and Russia. Nevertheless, he succeeded in wrecking an alliance

Hammer the Poles until they despair for their lives. I have every sympathy for their plight, but if we want to survive we have no choice but to exterminate them.
—OTTO VON BISMARCK

between these two nations. The diplomatic victory had a price, however: the Russians would now remain neutral if Austria or France went to war with Prussia.

Emperor Franz Josef of Austria then moved to reassert his authority in the German Confederation. He arranged a congress of all the ruling German princes, to meet in Frankfurt in August 1863. Wilhelm happened to be visiting the Austrian spa of Bad Gastein, so Franz Josef went there to deliver his invitation personally. Wilhelm felt greatly honored and very much wanted to attend — but Bismarck was also at Bad Gastein, keeping a watchful eye over the king of Prussia. The prime minister immediately realized that the Frankfurt congress was a trap. Franz Josef, with the backing of the lesser German princes, would use the occasion to tighten Austrian control of the German Confederation and confirm Prussia's status as a lesser power.

In no uncertain terms, Bismarck urged Wilhelm to reject the invitation. He followed the king to the

A cartoon satirizing the Danish War of 1864. That year Prussia and Austria created an alliance to reclaim the duchies of Schleswig and Holstein from Denmark, which, by annexing Schleswig in 1863, had violated German treaty rights. Prussia and Austria would ultimately go to war between themselves over the fate of the two duchies.

German state of Baden, all the while arguing and cajoling. At Baden, however, Wilhelm received another personal invitation from a messenger, who was none other than King John of Saxony, acting as the envoy of Franz Josef and all the German royalty.

Wilhelm was awestruck by this dazzling honor. "Thirty reigning princes and a king as their courier!" he exclaimed again and again. Bismarck now had to marshal all his powers of persuasion. He threatened to resign. He warned that Franz Josef was trying to reduce Prussia to a province of the Austrian Empire. Bismarck pleaded and raged until nearly 11:00 at night. Finally, the exhausted king, sprawled on a sofa and reduced to tears, agreed not to go to Frankfurt.

Bismarck immediately bolted out of the room, slamming the door with such violence that he wrenched off the handle. In a rage, he descended on King John's minister, Count Friedrich von Beust. "You have come to ruin us! You will not succeed!" Bismarck shouted, and handed over Wilhelm's note rejecting the invitation. Beust soothingly replied that King John would remain in Baden for a while, just to give Wilhelm time to think further about the matter. "If King John has not left by 6:00 tomorrow morning, then by 8:00 a Prussian battalion will move into Baden," Bismarck shot back. "Before my king is out of bed, King John's house will be surrounded by troops with only one order—that no Saxon is to be admitted."

Beust was incredulous. Bismarck had threatened to commit an unprovoked act of war against two sovereign states — Baden and Saxony. The Prussian prime minister would stop at nothing to get his way. "Breaches of law and peace are matters of perfect indifference to me," he proclaimed. "All I care for is the well-being of my king and country." Bismarck had made an enemy of Saxony, but he had also outmaneuvered Franz Josef. Without Prussian participation, the Frankfurt congress became a meaningless charade.

Bismarck was finally able to force a showdown with Austria over the small northern provinces of

These chatterboxes cannot really govern Prussia. . . . They know as little about politics as we knew in our student days — no, less! As far as foreign politics are concerned they are children.
—OTTO VON BISMARCK
on the members of
parliament in 1863

Schleswig and Holstein. Holstein was inhabited by Germans; the population of Schleswig was part German, part Danish. Under the Treaty of London, drawn up in 1852, the two duchies were ruled by the Danish king, though they could not actually become part of Denmark. In 1863, however, the new Danish king, Christian IX, formally annexed Schleswig.

Throughout Germany, indignant nationalists attacked this violation of treaty rights. The Holsteiners refused to recognize the Danish king and proposed German-bred Prince Friedrich of Augustenberg to rule the "Elbe duchies," as the two provinces were called. Privately, Bismarck could not have cared less about the duchies. "It is no concern of ours whether the Germans of Holstein are happy,"

In the war with Austria, the chief of the Prussian army general staff, Helmuth von Moltke, proved an extraordinarily skillful military strategist. Taking full advantage of Prussia's rail system, he kept his forces mobile and ready to attack at any moment from many directions.

he boldly remarked. But he realized that the crisis could be exploited to his own advantage. Wilhelm was frequently shocked by Bismarck's cold-bloodedness. German patriots were demanding a war of national liberation on behalf of Prince Friedrich. Bismarck would be happy to conquer Schleswig and Holstein—not for Friedrich, but for Prussia.

Bismarck quickly patched up relations with Austria and secured a formal alliance. Neither side had made many demands on the other; their agreement, signed in January of 1864, was specifically aimed at defeating Denmark. In February 1864 German and Austrian armies overran Schleswig and Holstein. On June 1 Prince Friedrich met Bismarck in Berlin, expecting to receive title to his new realm. To his dismay he learned that Bismarck would only allow him to reign as a Prussian pawn, and the prince declined to accept those humiliating terms. Denmark ceased fighting in August and surrendered to Austria and Prussia in October 1864. In September 1865 Bismarck was rewarded with the title of Count Bismarck-Schönhausen.

Two years later, as if the alliance with Austria had never existed, Bismarck would launch a war designed to rid Prussia of the Austrian challenge. That war would be a vital piece in the puzzle of German unification that Bismarck was putting together. That autumn, before the final confrontation with Austria, Bismarck had a last romantic interlude in Biarritz with Katharina Orlov. "It is like a dream to me," he wrote to Johanna. "There lies the sea in front of me, while Kathy works at her Beethoven overhead, such weather as we have not had all summer, and not a drop of ink in the house."

Returning to the world of diplomacy, Bismarck arranged the Convention of Gastein in August 1865. Under the treaty drawn up at this convention, Prussia occupied Schleswig and Lauenburg while Austria occupied Holstein. "I never imagined I should find an Austrian diplomat who would put his name to such a document!" Bismarck gloated, for indeed he had backed Austria into a corner. It could not hope to defend Holstein, a faraway province surrounded by the Prussian army. Inevitably,

Austria and Prussia would quarrel over the duchies, then war would break out, and Prussian troops would take over all of northern Germany. In addition, a trade quarrel that began in 1865 over continued Austrian resentment at being blocked from participation in the German Zollverein further made an alliance with Prussia impossible.

In October Bismarck visited Louis-Napoléon at Biarritz and made sure that the French emperor would stay neutral in any Austro-Prussian conflict. On April 8, 1866, Italy agreed to join Prussia in a war against Austria on two conditions. First, Italy would be rewarded with Venetia, an Italian-speaking province under Austrian rule. Second, the Italians would only fight if hostilities broke out within three months.

If Bismarck wanted a war, he was now racing a deadline. Count Alexander Mensdorff-Pouilly, who succeeded Rechberg as Austrian foreign minister, committed a fatal blunder. Mensdorff broke off negotiations with Prussia over the status of Schleswig and Holstein and on June 1 asked the German Confederation's Federal Diet to decide the future of the duchies. Bismarck denounced this action as a breach of the Gastein Convention and as unconstitutional. Prussian troops marched into Holstein on June 7, and the Austrians withdrew without a fight. Three days later, in need of another way of provoking the Austrians to fight, Bismarck defiantly declared an end to the German Confederation. On June 12, 1866, the Austrians and French secretly agreed that if they defeated the Prussians, Venetia would be handed over to France. On June 14 the Bundestag approved an Austrian motion to mobilize its armies against Prussia. The following day, the kingdoms of Hannover, Hesse-Cassel, and Saxony each received an ultimatum from Bismarck. If they did not cooperate with Prussia, they would be treated as enemies. Each refused to comply, and central Europe was plunged into war.

Bismarck knew that he was gambling everything on the outcome of the conflict. "If we are beaten . . . I shall die in the last charge," he promised a British diplomat. At first Austria, backed by several smaller

> *I feel that I've grown fifteen years older in this one year. People are even more stupid than I had thought.*
> —OTTO VON BISMARCK
> after one year as
> prime minister

German states, was generally expected to win. Eager to gain Venetia, French Emperor Louis-Napoléon urged the Italians to fight. The Italians mobilized their armies before the Prussians did and were soundly beaten by the Austrians.

Prussia had a valuable asset in what became known as the Seven Weeks' War in the chief of its army general staff, Helmuth von Moltke. Taking advantage of the latest developments in military technology, Moltke had planned the Austrian war with extraordinary precision. He would use the excellent Prussian railway network to move troops and supplies. Following strict timetables, Prussia could mobilize her armies four times faster than Austria. Moltke had equipped his infantry with the breech-loading "needle gun," which could fire five times faster than Austria's muzzle-loading rifles. Rather than follow the old-fashioned tactic of concentrating his forces, Moltke kept his armies divided and mobile. At the right moment these scattered units would pounce on the enemy from all sides. This strategy depended on perfect timing, but it allowed Moltke to command four separate armies while he sat by a telegraph key in a Berlin office.

Meeting little resistance, one of those armies swept through the smaller German states of Hannover, Saxony, and Hesse-Cassel. By July 2 two other columns, accompanied by Wilhelm and Bismarck, had cornered the Austrians at Königgrätz. A fourth army, led by Crown Prince Friedrich Wilhelm, had not yet joined with the king's forces, but Moltke decided to attack the following day.

At first, it was a closely fought battle, with terrible losses on both sides. The tide turned at 2:00 P.M., when the crown prince's army reached the battlefield and shattered the Austrian right flank. The Austrians lost about 40,000 men; the Prussians only 9,000. Even the iron-hearted Bismarck was shaken by the carnage. "If foreign ministers had always followed their sovereigns to the front, history would have fewer wars to tell of," he said some months later. "I have seen on a battlefield — and what is far worse, in the hospitals — the flower of

our youth carried off by wounds and disease; from this window I look down on the Wilhelmstrasse and see many a cripple who looks up and thinks that if that man up there had not made that wicked war I should be at home, healthy and strong."

After the Battle of Königgrätz King Wilhelm and Moltke were eager to march on Vienna and smash the Austrian Empire, but Bismarck, who had dragged Prussia into the war, did everything pos-

A detail from the painting *Battle of Königgrätz*. Nearly 50,000 men lost their lives in this famous battle, which was fought in July 1866. The Prussians defeated the Austrians, but Bismarck was so revolted by the violence and bloodshed that he moved to negotiate an end to the war.

63

With the victory at König-grätz, Bismarck was able to strengthen his own political position and successfully exclude Austria from any significant influence in future German affairs. The French Emperor Louis-Napoléon now stood as the last obstacle to German unity.

sible to stop it. In the end the crown prince persuaded his father to follow Bismarck's advice.

The war had already upset the European balance of power. The longer it lasted, the greater the risk that France or Russia might intervene to halt Prussian expansion. Realpolitik meant knowing where to stop. Bismarck, therefore, arranged a generous peace settlement, the Treaty of Prague, signed on August 23, 1866. Except for Venetia, which went to Italy, Austria lost no territory. It did, however, surrender all its influence in Germany. The German Confederation was dissolved, and Prussia absorbed Schleswig and Holstein, Hannover, Hesse-Cassel, and Frankfurt, all the territories north of the Main

River. Prussia had successfully undermined Austria's power, and Bismarck had gained extensive influence over Prussian politics. The day on which the Austrian army was crushed at Königgrätz, parliamentary elections were also held. Moderate liberals had left the Progressive party to form the National Liberal party. The liberal movement was now divided, and Bismarck faced much less opposition to his policies. He had, after all, decisively beaten Prussia's chief rival while serving German nationalism. It seemed he was taming the parliament he so strongly resented.

Bismarck had ensured that the Austrians would not oppose Prussia in any future conflicts by granting them lenient terms. Yet Austria was now isolated, cut off from German affairs, and the German Confederation was no more. Bismarck could now safely confront the last obstacle to German unity — Louis-Napoléon. Having failed to stop Bismarck, the emperor now found himself faced with an enlarged German state, no less powerful than France. As the French politician Louis-Adolphe Thiers remarked, "It is France who has been beaten at Sadowa [Königgrätz]."

The Austrian war did not take place because the existence of Prussia was threatened or in obedience to public opinion or the will of the people. It was a war prepared with deliberation . . . to secure and establish Prussian domination in Europe.
—HELMUTH VON MOLTKE
Prussian general

5

The Decisive Gamble

Königgrätz was also a defeat for German democracy. Before the battle, Bismarck's political position had been precarious. He had only a small base of a support in the Prussian parliament, where the liberal majority relentlessly attacked his foreign policy. An eminent judge, Rudolf von Thering, had denounced the assault on Austria as a "violation of every legal and moral principle. . . . I doubt whether a war has ever been provoked so shamelessly and with such horrifying frivolity."

That was before Königgrätz. After that victory, most Prussian liberals praised Bismarck to the skies. Suddenly they saw the virtues of blood and iron. Where years of parliamentary debate and newspaper articles had failed to unite Germany, realpolitik was succeeding. Now Thering cheerfully cast away his moral outrage. "I bow before the genius of Bismarck, who has achieved a masterpiece of political planning and action that has few parallels in history," he wrote. "I have forgiven the man

What is an opportunist? He is a man who uses the most favorable opportunity to carry through what he regards as useful and appropriate.
—OTTO VON BISMARCK

An 1867 portrait of Bismarck by Hermann Romer. Explaining the likelihood of German victory in a conflict with France, Bismarck said,"The Germans play the part rather of a man, the Romance peoples that of a woman. A man often falls, but he can always pick himself up; a woman, once fallen, cannot recover."

everything he has done up to now; moreover, I have convinced myself that it was necessary. What seemed to us, the uninitiated, to be criminal arrogance turns out to have been the indispensable means to the end."

If the liberals of Prussia had not been so indecisive — or if the kings of Prussia had not chosen to rely on the cold genius of Bismarck — then, with time, Germany might have evolved into a democracy. However, Bismarck could now count on the support of the new National Liberal party, which was willing to sacrifice liberal principles for the cause of national unity. "I have beaten them all!" he exulted, pounding the table in triumph.

British historian A. J. P. Taylor explains: "He never became identified with any cause, whether monarchy or German nationalism. . . . This gave him freedom to manoeuvre."

In September 1866, at the height of his popularity, Bismarck almost suffered a breakdown. His long hours of work and constant battles with his many enemies led to nervous exhaustion. Johanna took him to the Baltic seashore to recover. For his services to Prussia he was awarded the rank of major general and 400,000 *Talers*. With this windfall he purchased Varzin, a huge estate in the forests of Pomerania in Prussia.

By December 1867 he was back in Berlin, fully recovered and busy steering the ship of state. Eight days later — so quickly that hardly anyone had a chance to argue — he produced a draft of a constitution for a new North German Confederation. Under this charter Prussia was master of the northern German states, and the chancellor — Bismarck — was master of Prussia. He created a federal council that could make laws and a parliament that was merely a rubber stamp. The council served the princes who ruled the various northern states. To satisfy liberal politicians, Bismarck's constitution gave the vote and the right to a secret ballot to peasants as well as landlords. The king of Hannover was deposed and his large private fortune was confiscated by the Prussian government. Bismarck could now draw on this huge fortune "to pursue the reptiles into their lair." The "reptile fund," as it came to be known, was used to bribe newspapers, politicians, and even, on one occasion, a king.

Four independent southern German states — Bavaria, Baden, Württemberg, and Hesse-Darmstadt — still remained beyond Prussia's grasp. These kingdoms might join a united Germany if Bismarck could engineer a war with France, but he would not fire the first shot. He was prepared to bide his time until Louis-Napoléon stumbled into war. "The gift of waiting while a situation develops is an essential requirement of practical politics," he wrote.

He would wait more than three years. In September 1868 Queen Isabella II of Spain was deposed after a successful local revolution. Bismarck at once saw an opportunity to provoke the French, who were trying to put their candidate on the throne. He dispatched his agents to Madrid, and by September 1869 he knew that the Spanish crown had been offered to Prince Leopold of Hohenzollern-Sigmaringen. In June 1870, after weeks of relentless badgering, Bismarck persuaded Wilhelm to support Leopold's candidacy. Leopold was not only the favorite of German liberals, but as king of Spain he might block French ambitions in the region. The long fuse had been lit. Triumphant and exhausted, Bismarck retired to Varzin to wait for the explosion.

The Cortes, Spain's parliament, was supposed to confer the crown on Leopold, in secret, on or about June 20. Before he could do anything about it, Louis-Napoléon would soon read in the newspapers that a Hohenzollern was king of Spain. That, at least, was Bismarck's plan. However, owing to an error in decoding a telegram concerning the Spanish envoy's return from Berlin, the Cortes delegates were sent home before they could vote on Leopold. On July 2 the secret leaked out.

The French were furious. On July 6 Duke Agenor of Gramont, Louis-Napoléon's foreign minister, proclaimed that "the interests and the honor of France are now in peril." Bismarck was clearly disturbed by this unexpected turn of events. "This looks like

Struggle is everywhere, without struggle no life, and if we want to go on living, we must be ready for further struggle.
—OTTO VON BISMARCK

The Prussians suffered numerous losses against the French at the Battle of Saint-Privat, and among the wounded were Bismarck's two sons, Herbert (pictured here) and Bill. When he heard the news Bismarck rode 20 miles on horseback to assure himself of the safety of the two young men.

war," he gravely remarked, but he was still prepared to let France begin the fighting. For the time being, he mobilized only the German newspapers, which launched a campaign against the French.

For several days Bismarck coolly allowed tensions to build. On both sides politicians delivered angry speeches, journalists demanded war, diplomatic telegrams were shot back and forth. Bismarck had neglected to keep an eye on the king, who was away in Ems doing everything possible to assure the French that he wanted peace. On July 12 Wilhelm managed to secure the withdrawal of Prince Leopold's candidacy.

When the news reached Bismarck, he was dining with Moltke and Roon. The "humiliation" of Ems plunged him into a deep depression, and he talked of resigning. He quickly recovered, however, when he realized that he still might push the French into declaring war. He saw to it that the duke of Gramont received the news about Leopold not from Wilhelm directly but through ordinary diplomatic channels. Just as Bismarck had hoped, the hotheaded duke felt deeply insulted by this treatment and demanded from Wilhelm a formal "assurance that he [would] not authorize a renewal of the candidacy." Wilhelm, in turn, was insulted by this ultimatum, which implied that his word could not be trusted. He refused to grant any such assurance, whereupon Gramont insisted that Wilhelm apologize for having supported Leopold's candidacy in the first place.

On the evening of July 13 Bismarck received the dispatch from Ems recounting Wilhelm's encounter with Benedetti, the French ambassador. He did not actually rewrite the contents of Wilhelm's message, but by cutting out a few soothing words, he made it more to the point.

The next day was Bastille Day, the national holiday of France. The newspapers of Paris trumpeted war. Mobs in the streets cried "On to Berlin!" and the French armed forces were mobilized. Both sides, remembering the conquests of the first Emperor Napoleon, expected the war to begin with a French thrust into Germany. Even Wilhelm did not think his officers would need maps of France for some time.

But the French army was far less efficient than the Prussian war machine. As in 1866, Moltke mobilized his soldiers with breathtaking speed. Dividing his forces into three armies, he launched a series of coordinated assaults that immediately threw the French off balance.

Bismarck and the king left for the front on July 31. The chancellor was amused to find that the French people regarded him as an evil monster. "The old women when they hear my name fall to their knees and plead with me to spare their lives," he wrote home to Johanna. "Attila was a lamb compared with me!" The Prussians suffered some serious losses in the early Battle of Saint-Privat, and among those reported wounded were Bismarck's two sons, Herbert and Bill. In a panic Bismarck rode more than 20 miles to find them. Both, he joyfully discovered, were injured but alive. The chancellor accompanied Wilhelm into dangerous circumstances. On one occasion he had to give the king's horse a kick when the king brought himself and the chancellor too close to enemy fire.

After only a few days of fighting, Louis-Napoléon lost his nerve. On August 7, 1870, he ordered half

Bismarck rides to meet Louis-Napoléon in September 1870, following the French surrender at Sedan and the French ruler's capture by Moltke. Notwithstanding such setbacks, a provisional government, led by Jules Favre, was created in Paris, and the French resistance continued.

his army to retreat to the fortress town of Metz, where it was bottled up by Moltke's forces until surrendering on October 27. On September 1, at the Battle of Sedan, the remainder of the French army was destroyed. The following day Louis-Napoléon was taken prisoner by Moltke.

The war did not end at that point. French resistance continued in Paris, the French capital, where a provisional government, led initially by Jules Favre and Léon Gambetta, took the place of the emperor. The Prussians laid siege to the city, and Gambetta organized the countryside to resist the invaders.

Frenchmen were no longer willing to fight for a corrupt emperor, but they raised ragtag armies and tried to break the siege of Paris. *Francs-tireurs* (guerrillas) harried the Germans behind the front lines.

More swiftly than anyone had imagined possible, without taking a single false step, Bismarck had overcome Prussia's most powerful enemies and

THE BETTMANN ARCHIVE

made himself master of Germany. Only now, at the very pinnacle of his success, did his keen sense of realpolitik begin to falter. It seemed he forgot his own statement that foreign policy should be free from "dislike or affection for foreign states and their governments."

His first error was the peace he imposed. The French expected that he would treat them leniently, as he had the Austrians. After Sedan, Bismarck privately remarked that France would only have to surrender two strategic strongholds, Metz and Strasbourg. But on September 18 he confronted Favre, the new French foreign minister, with much harsher terms. Germany, Bismarck asserted, had been the victim of unprovoked French aggression. He demanded the entire border region of Alsace-Lorraine as a buffer territory against future attacks.

Favre was stunned. Although some inhabitants of Alsace-Lorraine were German speaking, such a concession would place many Frenchmen under German rule. "You want to destroy France!" cried Favre, and he returned to Paris to continue the war.

Bismarck had demanded such terms with good reason. Moltke and Wilhelm, in the flush of victory, wanted to crush France completely, just as they had wanted to crush Austria in 1866. Bismarck had resisted this idea. Bismarck detested democratic rule but he did not favor marching on Paris. Without Louis-Napoléon, the new French republic was in turmoil, and Bismarck would have preferred "to leave these people to stew in their own juice." (Indeed, in March 1871, when the French National Assembly accepted the need to surrender, the National Guard, composed mainly of workers, started a bloody revolt against the Third Republic—as the French national government after Louis-Napoléon was called—known as the "Paris Commune." The republic defeated the revolutionaries at a high cost.) Bismarck did not press the matter with Moltke, whose troops swiftly surrounded Paris. At home, German newspapers demanded nothing less than Alsace-Lorraine. Perhaps Bismarck thought that the French, trapped in a hopeless military situation, would accept any terms he dictated. Instead, they fought on.

Unwilling to accept France's surrender to Germany and the harsh peace terms, working class, socialist, and republican Parisians rebelled against the Third Republic in March 1871. Known as the Paris Commune, the insurrection was suppressed, but not before a great deal of blood was shed.

Yes, Bismarck has made us great and powerful, but he has robbed us of our friends, the sympathies of the world, and — our conscience.
—CROWN PRINCE FRIEDRICH

THE BETTMANN ARCHIVE

A Prussian battery fires on Paris in 1871. Frenchmen rallied and formed militia units in a desperate attempt to break the siege of the capital. Bismarck, in turn, ordered all such guerrillas captured and executed; villages that had offered the militiamen refuge were burned.

Bismarck grew increasingly frustrated and angry. The French had completely upset his timetable. They could not possibly win, so why were they dragging out the war? According to the principles of realpolitik it made no sense, but Bismarck's rational political outlook had failed to account for love of country. He ordered the execution of captured francs-tireurs. Villages that had offered the guerrillas safe haven were burned. He even talked of deporting French civilians to German concentration camps. When Paris refused to surrender, Bismarck impatiently demanded that the city be shelled into submission. Moltke wisely refused. He knew that bombardment would only serve to stiffen Parisian resistance.

The war had at least induced Bavaria, Baden, Württemburg, and Hesse-Darmstadt to join a new unified German Empire. Wilhelm, however, stubbornly refused to accept the imperial crown. He did not care to give up his old title for a new one, especially if the latter was bestowed on him by what he considered a mob of common parliamentary politicians. Of course, if the offer was made by a fellow

king, then Wilhelm could hardly refuse. Not even the king was going to ruin Bismarck's grand design. Drawing on his "reptile fund," Bismarck bribed the mad King Ludwig II of Bavaria. In return for a yearly stipend of 300,000 marks, Ludwig wrote and signed a letter asking Wilhelm to become the German emperor. The Prussian king reluctantly agreed, having no idea that Bismarck was behind the letter.

The proclamation ceremony took place on January 18, 1871, at the Hall of Mirrors at the Palace of Versailles, the magnificent residence of the French monarchs built by Louis XIV. At the last minute there was a squabble over the exact wording of Wilhelm's new title. He wanted to be nothing less than "Emperor of Germany." His fellow German monarchs insisted on "German Emperor," implying that although Wilhelm was German *and* an emperor, he was not necessarily emperor of all Germany. The impasse was resolved when he was simply proclaimed emperor as "Kaiser Wilhelm." In any case, no other German king bothered to attend the ceremony. Wilhelm was so furious that he would not even shake hands with Bismarck. The chancellor

Wilhelm of Prussia is proclaimed kaiser, January 18, 1871, at the Palace of Versailles, France. The ceremonious creation of the new German Empire was somewhat of a farce; the call for Wilhelm to take on the new title was bought for 300,000 marks, and no other German king bothered to attend.

On January 28, 1871, the French agreed to an armistice. Pictured is a triumphant Bismarck with French statesmen Louis-Adolphe Thiers and Jules Favre, meeting to discuss the terms of the peace agreement — terms that heavily burdened the French for many years.

was equally distressed. He announced his greatest triumph, the creation of the German Empire, with an evident lack of enthusiasm.

Ten days later the French agreed to an armistice. They had sacrificed everything to lift the siege of Paris and failed.

On February 21 Louis-Adolphe Thiers, now the head of the French government, arrived at Versailles to negotiate a peace treaty. Bismarck brusquely stated his demands and threatened to resume the war if Thiers did not give in. The French were burdened with an indemnity of 5 billion francs. They managed to pay off that penalty by 1873, but they would never be reconciled to the loss of Alsace-Lorraine.

"The war represents the German revolution, a greater political event than the French Revolution of the last century," proclaimed British statesman Benjamin Disraeli. "There is not a diplomatic tradition which has not been swept away," he solemnly added. "The balance of power has been entirely destroyed." In the center of the continent, Bismarck had created an empire with the most powerful army in the world. In all Europe, only Russia had a larger population than Germany. Only Britain had a larger industrial base, and the Germans were rapidly closing that gap.

To become so powerful, however, Germany had paid a terrible price. On the last day of 1870 Crown Prince Friedrich observed that Bismarck's triumph of realpolitik had been a terrible moral defeat. "We are no longer looked upon as the innocent victims of wrong, but rather as arrogant victors, no longer content with the conquest of the foe, but determined to bring about his utter ruin," he wrote in his diary. Once Germany had been admired as a "nation of thinkers and philosophers, poets and artists, idealists and enthusiasts," he wrote. Now the world saw it as "only a nation of conquerors and destroyers, to which no pledged word, no treaty, is sacred, and which speaks with rude insolence of those who have done it no injury. . . . We are neither loved nor respected, but only feared."

The proclamation of Wilhelm I as kaiser is portrayed in this painting entitled *Apotheosis of Wilhelm I*, by Ferdinand Keller, as a mock deification, complete with cherubs and heavenly light. As chancellor, Bismarck dominated Wilhelm's 17-year reign as kaiser.

6

Dividing Germany Again

Most Germans did not share their crown prince's misgivings. They reveled in their newfound power. Bismarck, one newspaper said, could bask in "the iron radiance of a million bayonets." In March 1871 a grateful nation granted him the title of prince and a 17,000-acre estate at Friedrichsruh.

At home Bismarck's task was clear. He had to create a spirit of national unity. The German people, who until recently had owed their loyalties to several independent principalities, should be made to feel that they now belonged to a united German *Reich* (empire), ruled by the kaiser. But almost immediately after the war with France, Bismarck began antagonizing large sections of Germany's population. He systematically created deep social divisions within the nation he had unified politically.

His first target was the Roman Catholic church. Prussia and northern Germany were predominantly Protestant, but with the absorption of southern Germany and Alsace-Lorraine the empire now included a large Catholic minority. In 1870 a Vatican council declared that when speaking officially on

I am bored; the great things are done. The German Empire is made.
—OTTO VON BISMARCK

Calling Catholicism "a state within a state," Bismarck waged an attack on the Catholic church in Germany during the 1870s; he had laws enacted that diminished the power and independence of the church. Clergy who expressed opposition to the new laws were imprisoned.

questions of faith and morals, the pope (then Pius IX) is infallible. German Catholics organized the Center party, which in March 1871 won 58 seats in the lower house of the new imperial parliament, the *Reichstag*. Prussia retained control of the upper house, the *Bundesrat*. Despite this power, Bismarck's relations with the National Liberals were uneasy. Distrustful of parliament's role, he expected the majority party to follow him without question.

Bismarck had always harbored some anti-Catholic prejudices, and now all his bigotry surfaced. He suspected that German Catholics would be more loyal to the pope than to the German Empire. Bismarck commenced a campaign against the church with the support of the National Liberals, who called it the *Kulturkampf* — the battle of civilizations. In 1871 the Prussian government began to assert control over Catholic schools. In 1872 the Jesuits (a Catholic religious order with a tradition of loyalty to the pope and devotion to higher learning) were expelled from Germany. The May Laws of 1873 tried to bring the Catholic church under the domination of the Prussian government. On July 13, 1874, a Catholic cooper shot at the chancellor while he rode by in his carriage in Kissingen, where he was visiting the town's mineral spring. The assassin's bullet missed its mark, only grazing Bismarck's right hand. Bismarck wildly charged that the Center party was somehow responsible for the assassination attempt. To him, its members were *Reichsfeinde*, enemies of the reich.

The Kulturkampf was a disaster. Many German Catholics had resented the pope's assumption of infallibility, but in response to Bismarck's repression they rallied behind the church. In Prussia every Catholic bishop and more than half of the priests accepted imprisonment or loss of their congregations rather than submit to the government. The Center party, far from being eliminated, increased its representation to 94 seats in the 1874 elections and became a stronghold of opposition to Bismarck.

Meanwhile, Bismarck quarreled with his former allies, the National Liberals, over the government's finances. The emperor and his generals wanted a

Bismarck utterly misunderstands and underrates the power of the Church. Thinking himself more infallible than the pope, he cannot tolerate two infallibilities in Europe and fancies he can select and appoint the next pontiff as he would a Prussian general, who will carry out his orders to the Catholic clergy.

—LORD ODO RUSSELL
British ambassador
to Berlin

Kaiser Wilhelm I in 1871. Instead of working to create a spirit of unity within the newly created German Empire, Bismarck divided the German people by attempting to stifle Catholicism and socialism.

long-term military budget, which would allow them to plan defense policies without parliamentary interference. The liberals insisted on voting a new budget every three years; anything less would effectively eliminate any parliamentary control over the military. Bismarck eventually settled for a compromise that satisfied no one: the generals would receive a seven-year budget. The chancellor also asked for beer and sugar taxes and a government tobacco monopoly. Again the liberals refused. Bismarck still reigned supreme in military and foreign affairs but kept his hands off the German economy. He had not yet sought to bring government control into the economy.

To add to the chancellor's troubles, the German economy was in a depression. Immediately after the Franco-Prussian War, the national economy had soared in a frenzy of stock-market speculation, fueled in part by the huge reparations payments received from France. Beginning in 1873 a series of

Before I was a minister I had a large number of friends and very few enemies, even among my opponents; now it is the other way around.
—OTTO VON BISMARCK
in 1875

financial scandals coupled with stiff competition from British industry and U.S. agriculture battered German manufacturers and farmers alike.

The growth of German industry had increased the size of a new class of impoverished industrial workers. Rural laborers migrated to the cities, where they worked long hours for low wages, lived in overcrowded slums, and were frequently unemployed. Many of these workers joined labor unions and voted for the growing Social Democratic party, the German socialists.

Bismarck responded to the Social Democrats as he had to the Catholics — with repression. In 1876 he introduced a bill in the Reichstag that would have made it a crime to publish attacks on "the family, property, universal military service, or other foundations of public order, in such manner as to undermine morality, respect for law, or love of the fatherland." Although the Social Democrats were the target of this legislation, the liberals realized that it could also be used against them, and they voted it down. That same year, his alliance with the National Liberals remained strong, and he condemned the conservative newspaper *Kreuzzeitung*. Thirty years earlier he had been closely associated with the paper.

On May 11, 1878, an unemployed plumber fired a shot at Kaiser Wilhelm. He missed, but now Bismarck again had an excuse to demand an antisocialist law. Again the Reichstag refused. On June 2 there was another attempt on Wilhelm's life, and this time he was seriously wounded. In this tragedy Bismarck saw only another opportunity for political gain. "Now I've got those scoundrels where I want them!" he chortled. He meant the National Liberals. He suddenly turned on them, publicly charging that they had failed to protect their emperor from socialist murderers. (It did not matter that neither of the would-be assassins was a member of the Social Democratic party.) The liberals lost much ground to the Conservative party in the 1878 elections.

Stunned by this setback, many liberals voted for the antisocialist bill, which was finally passed in October. The law banned the Social Democrats and

> *Bismarck is more necessary than I am.*
> —KAISER WILHELM I

A cartoon from the British magazine *Punch* satirizing Bismarck's antisocialist bill. Passed in 1878, the legislation banned all socialist organizations and publications but still did not slow the growth of the Social Democratic party.

all other socialist organizations. Most newspapers, publishers, and booksellers that published socialist writings were shut down.

Socialist literature, however, could still be imported into Germany from Switzerland. Although many urban socialist leaders were exiled to the countryside, they continued their agitation in rural areas. Social Democratic candidates could still be elected to the Reichstag, and the party actually increased its representation from 12 seats in 1877 to 35 seats in 1890.

Faced with this impasse, Bismarck abruptly reversed his domestic policies in 1879. After negotiations with Pope Leo XIII, Pius IX's successor, he scrapped the Kulturkampf and deserted many of the liberals who had supported it. Now he forged a new parliamentary alliance, which included the Conservative party, some liberals, and his old enemy the Center party. This governing coalition enacted tariffs to protect agriculture and industry, and soon the German economy was booming again. The German Empire now had the "powerful, unshakable financial foundation" Bismarck thought it needed. In 1880 he became minister of commerce.

Bismarck also adopted a new strategy for dealing with radicals and possible revolution. In 1881 he stunned the Reichstag by calling for the creation of the world's first welfare state. The government, he affirmed, should offer the poor "a helping hand in distress. . . . Not as alms, but as a right." By 1889 the Reichstag had granted German workers national health, accident, and disability insurance as well as retirement pensions. At that time no other government provided these services.

Bismarck's domestic policies were consistent with the doctrine of *Realpolitik* he had pursued in foreign affairs — any alliance could be broken, any program abandoned, any supporter betrayed in the ultimate struggle for power.

THE BETTMANN ARCHIVE

Bismarck hoped to steal the Social Democrats' thunder by creating what he himself called a system of "state socialism." He was shrewd enough to see that the German worker would not overthrow the government that offered him social security. "Whoever has a pension assured to him for his old age is much more contented and easier to manage than the man who has no such prospect," the chancellor explained. Liberal economics emphasized individual freedom. To Bismarck the power of the state was more important. True, a welfare state would be expensive, but it might "avert a revolution" — and that, said Bismarck, "is a good investment for our money."

These measures did not halt the growth of the Social Democratic party, but now that the German workers had their pensions to protect, they did become more moderate in their demands. Socialists gradually abandoned revolutionary goals and turned to bread-and-butter issues such as better wages and working conditions.

Bismarck's welfare state, like his policies toward Catholics and liberals, reflected the application of realpolitik on the domestic front. He was prepared to adopt any program that enhanced his power and to abandon any program that did not work. To achieve his ends, he was always ready to reverse his tactics, betray his friends, or cooperate with his enemies. In 1848 he had fought the German nationalists; then he turned around and supported German unity when it became clear that he could be the leader of a united Germany. Bismarck could even embrace specific socialist ideas — so long as he controlled the system.

The great conservative became the greatest of innovators.
—A. J. P. TAYLOR
British historian,
on Bismarck

7

The Conductor of Europe

After 1871 Bismarck's foreign policy goals were simple and straightforward. Germany, he declared, now had all the territory it needed. From here on it only wanted to preserve the peace and the stability of Europe. France, he realized, would never rest until it had recovered Alsace-Lorraine, but it was too weak to fight Germany alone. Bismarck therefore had to establish good relations with all the other European powers to ensure that France acquired no strong allies. For the most part he succeeded in maintaining this delicate diplomatic balance despite some startling political blunders.

Bismarck now reaped benefits from the generous peace he had granted to Austria in 1866. Austria-Hungary (Austria had joined its empire with the kingdom of Hungary in 1867) had remained neutral during the Franco-Prussian War. In 1871 Kaiser Wilhelm paid a friendly visit to Emperor Franz Josef, while Bismarck negotiated with the foreign minister of Austria-Hungary. Franz Josef accepted an invitation to visit Berlin in September 1872 — and then, quite by surprise, Tsar Alexander II of Russia invited himself to the German capital at the same time.

It is not easy to be emperor under such a chancellor.
—KAISER WILHELM I
on Bismarck

Bismarck's gargantuan appetite for food and drink equaled his insatiable lust for power. He suffered numerous physical ailments because of his years of gluttony, and in 1877 his doctors warned him that he could die within the year.

THE UNIFICATION OF GERMANY

- Kingdom of Prussia before 1866
- Acquired 1866–1867
- Acquired 1871

Map showing the evolution of Germany in the 19th century from many independent states to a single nation. After the defeat of France in the Franco-Prussian War, the southern German states joined the members of the North German Confederation, and the German Empire was established in 1871.

When the three monarchs met, Bismarck jumped at the opportunity to cement an alliance. In 1873 the *Dreikaiserbund*, the Three Emperors' League, was agreed to in Vienna.

Bismarck considered the league his greatest diplomatic triumph, but it had serious weaknesses. It was not a true alliance. The signatories had merely agreed to quell revolutionary movements and consult if another nation threatened war.

Also, Bismarck was never able to entice the world's leading power into an alliance. Great Britain had come to fear Germany ever since Bismarck's war on France. Protected by her formidable navy, the British were committed to a policy of "splendid isolation." So long as no other power threatened its vital interests or tried to upset the European balance of power, Britain would not join any entangling alliances. Instead of respecting this viewpoint, Bismarck, who claimed to be bored in 1874, antagonized the British. Benjamin Disraeli perceived the Three Emperors' League as a threat to European peace, particularly since it included Russia, Britain's archenemy.

Bismarck confirmed those fears by needlessly provoking a war scare in 1875. France had paid off her war reparations and was rapidly rebuilding her army. Moltke and Bismarck began to spread rumors about a possible attack on the nation that had surrendered to the Germans only four years earlier. On April 8 European diplomats were shocked by a front-page headline in a Berlin newspaper that read "Is War in Sight?" The kaiser was frantic. War was the last thing he wanted. Bismarck assured Wilhelm and the world that he desired only peace. In fact, everyone except the emperor knew that Bismarck had planted the inflammatory article.

This attempt to manufacture an international crisis looked foolish. One diplomat asked Moltke what he would do with another victory over France. "I don't know," said Moltke with a sigh. "That would surely be most embarrassing." Bismarck may never have intended to fight the French; perhaps he was only trying to intimidate them into halting their rearmament program.

In any case, the plot backfired. At a Berlin dinner party on April 21, one of Bismarck's assistants told the French ambassador that Germany would be entirely justified in starting a war. The ambassador reported those remarks to the French foreign minister, who passed them on to the governments of Europe and the London *Times*. When the news broke, Britain and Italy issued warnings to Germany. Prince Alexander Gorchakov, the chancellor of Russia, personally asked Bismarck to promise that he had no plans to invade France. The chancellor had no choice but to give that assurance.

"Bismarck has put European opinion to the test and now he has got his answer," declared the British foreign secretary, Edward Stanley, Lord Derby. The clumsily orchestrated war scare caused the

> *It was a psychological necessity for Bismarck to make his power felt by tormenting, harassing, mistreating people. His pessimistic view of life, which had long ago blighted every human pleasure, left him with only one source of amusement, and future historians must recognize that the Bismarck regime was a constant orgy of scorn and abuse of mankind.*
> —FRIEDRICH VON HOLSTEIN
> German diplomat

THE BETTMANN ARCHIVE

British Prime Minister Benjamin Disraeli in 1878, the year he and Bismarck met at the Congress of Berlin, where a settlement of the recent Balkan crisis was negotiated. Disraeli found Bismarck's congratulations on Britain's acquisition of Cyprus inappropriate.

No one, not even the most malevolent democrat, has any idea how much nullity and charlatanism is in diplomacy.
—OTTO VON BISMARCK

other great powers to regard Germany as the greatest threat to continental peace. They would no longer allow Bismarck to threaten others with impunity. Angry and frustrated, he asked his emperor for permission to resign in 1877.

When Wilhelm appeared ready to grant his request, Bismarck quickly settled instead for a long rest from his duties. The vacation hardly restored Bismarck's spirits. He was saddened by the death of Katharina Orlov (at age 35), and his own health was collapsing. "My doctors threaten me with death within the year if I don't completely pull out of all business," he complained to Katharina's widowed husband. "I myself thirst after peace and am filled with an irresistible longing . . . to live out the days remaining to me in total seclusion."

Actually, Bismarck could not bear inactivity, nor would the pressures of diplomacy allow him to rest. In the Balkans, several oppressed Christian peoples — Serbs, Romanians, Bulgarians, Macedonians, and Greeks — were challenging the brutal domination of the Muslim Ottoman Empire (Turkey). If and when Ottoman rule collapsed, both Austria-Hungary and Russia were prepared to intervene. The Russians hoped to accomplish a long-standing goal of their foreign policy by capturing a port on the eastern Mediterranean. Britain and France, however, feared that Russian expansion would threaten the Suez Canal, their vital sea link to Asia.

Germany had no interests in the Balkans. "It's not worth the healthy bones of a single Pomeranian musketeer," Bismarck declared. However, he did not want Austria-Hungary and Russia to fight each other over the region, so he urged his two allies to divide the Balkans into two spheres of influence.

Such an agreement was reached, and in April 1877 Russia went to war with the Ottoman Empire. Tsar Alexander II's troops liberated Romania and Bulgaria and by January 1878 had reached the outskirts of Constantinople (now Istanbul, Turkey). Greatly alarmed, Prime Minister Disraeli sent the British fleet to check the Russians at the Dardanelles, the narrow strait separating the European continent from Turkey. On March 3 the Ottoman Empire was forced by the Russians to sign the Treaty of San Stefano, which added territory to Bulgaria, expanding its border to the Aegean Sea. Bulgaria was a client state of Russia, and the tsar had in effect won the outlet on the Mediterranean he had wanted since the Crimean War.

In the spring of 1878 the British made two secret treaties: one with Russia and one with Turkey. Russia agreed not to base its fleet in the Aegean; Britain made a security agreement with Turkey, promising to protect Turkey's eastern frontier. Some Balkan territory was returned to the Ottoman Empire. Britain, represented in the negotiations by Prime Minister Benjamin Disraeli, acquired the island of Cyprus. Congratulating Disraeli, Bismarck stated, "This is progress! It will be popular: a nation loves progress!" Disraeli was not flattered. "His idea of progress was evidently seizing something," he tartly remarked.

To avoid being completely excluded from the Balkan Peninsula, Austria-Hungary also obtained an agreement from Britain. Under pressure from Bismarck, Austria-Hungary suggested that the great powers should meet in Berlin to negotiate a formally recognized revision of the Treaty of San Stefano.

Statesmen from Russia, Austria-Hungary, the Ottoman Empire, Britain, France, Italy, and Germany convened the Congress of Berlin on June 13, 1878. Bismarck reluctantly agreed to chair the conference as an "honest broker." (However, Bismarck's own banker seemed skeptical when he said, "There are no honest brokers.") It would be a delicate job, for he would have to mediate a settlement without alienating any of the participants, especially his allies Austria-Hungary and Russia. The final treaty satisfied Austria, which was allowed to occupy the neighboring province of Bosnia-Herzegovina. The Russians were not happy with the settlement, however. They were allowed to acquire some territorial spoils, but Bulgaria was divided, effectively denying Russia a port on the Aegean Sea. Having expected German support at Berlin, Tsar Alexander com-

> *Colonial policy is not made by generals and royal councillors but by trading firms and travelling salesmen.*
> —OTTO VON BISMARCK

A painting by Anton von Werner depicting the Congress of Berlin, June 13, 1878. At left, seated, is the Russian chancellor, Prince Aleksandr Gorchakov, with British Prime Minister Disraeli. Chairman and host of the conference, Bismarck (center, foreground), greets the Russian ambassador to Berlin, Count Pyotr Shuvalov.

plained that the Congress had been "a European coalition against Russia under the leadership of Prince Bismarck."

Bismarck had worked with other diplomats to thwart the ambitions of the Russians. In so doing, he had preserved the peace but had turned his back on the tsar and broken the Three Emperors' League. With Austria-Hungary and Russia competing in the Balkans, Bismarck always found it difficult to maintain cordial relations with both nations. Now his sleep was disturbed by a new nightmare — the fear that France and Russia would join forces and attack Germany on two fronts.

The essence of Bismarck's diplomatic strategy had always been to play off one nation against another. By promoting mutual fears and rivalries among the various European powers, he drove them into Germany's arms and was able to preserve a balance of power that enabled Germany to remain the strongest nation on the continent. In October 1879 Germany and Austria-Hungary concluded an alliance, the Reinsurance Treaty, each promising to aid the other against an attack by Russia. Kaiser

Wilhelm, an uncle of the tsar, at first refused to authorize this break with Russia, but once again Bismarck wore down his resistance.

The pact was designed to frighten the tsar into patching up his differences with Bismarck — and it succeeded. The Russians, suddenly finding themselves diplomatically isolated, confronting the threat of a German–Austro-Hungarian coalition, abruptly turned around and asked Bismarck to revive the Three Emperors' League. He was happy to comply, but Austria-Hungary objected to an alliance with its Russian rivals. Bismarck then began using the same strategy on Austria-Hungary. He supported the tsar's ambitions in the Balkans until Austria-Hungary gave in. Tsar Alexander II was assassinated on March 13, 1881. Alexander III, his openly anti-German son, succeeded him. Nevertheless, on June 18, 1881, Austria-Hungary, Germany, and Russia revived the Three Emperors' League. This time, each promised to remain neutral if any of the others went to war with a fourth nation (excluding the Ottoman Empire).

Italy also wanted to join forces with Germany — but not with Austria. Rome coveted the Austrian territories of Trentino and Trieste, which had large Italian populations. Bismarck, however, had already started a diplomatic maneuver that would eventually bring Italy into a German–Austro-Hungarian alliance. At the Congress of Berlin he had secretly promised France the Ottoman province of Tunis (now known as Tunisia), even though Italy had important interests there. When French troops, led by Jules Ferry, seized Tunis in 1881, the Italians were outraged. They had wanted to seize Tunis for themselves. Without a strong army and an industrial economy, Italy could not compete with Europe's other powers independently. The Italians would have to find allies. In 1882 Italy joined Austria-Hungary and Germany in forming the Triple Alliance. Bismarck had only contempt for his Italian allies, stating, "They have such a large appetite, and such poor teeth." Through the alliance, however, the chancellor was able once more to isolate France.

During this period his health seriously deteriorated. "The only recreation in my overworked existence is to talk about foreign affairs," he once complained. All his life he had eaten and drunk too much. At meals Johanna did nothing to discourage his gluttony, and when he developed a stomachache she treated it with generous servings of *pâté de foie gras* (goose liver pâté). He suffered from insomnia, jaundice, influenza, neuralgia, rheumatism, migraine headaches, gout, gallstones, varicose veins, shingles, and piles. In 1883, at age 68, he was diagnosed by his physicians as having cancer.

Johanna consulted another doctor, or at least someone who called himself a doctor. Ernst Schweninger was a rather shady practitioner who had been stripped of his medical license, but he knew the right treatment for Bismarck. He commanded his patient to follow a very strict diet, to avoid alcohol, and to sleep regular hours. Schweninger was perhaps the only man who ever succeeded in making Bismarck follow orders. The chancellor lost nearly 60 pounds, and some of his vigor returned. The cancer diagnosis turned out to be false. Bismarck rewarded Schweninger by making him a professor of medicine at the University of Berlin, ignoring the protests of the faculty.

Revitalized, Bismarck now focused on the issue of colonial expansion. In the 1880s Britain, France, Italy, Belgium, and Portugal were all competing to establish colonies in Africa. At first Bismarck refused to enter Germany into the race for colonies. What was the point of acquiring a few worthless patches of African jungle? he asked. Such a policy would only bring Germany into conflict with the world's greatest imperial power—Britain.

In Germany, however, there was a growing public clamor for colonies. Businessmen needed new markets and sources of raw materials. Missionaries wanted to convert the natives to Christianity. In 1884 the explorer Karl Peters staked out 60,000 square miles of east Africa for Germany. Naval officers also believed that Germany should acquire

Undoubtedly I have caused unhappiness for many. But for me three great wars would not have taken place, eighty thousand men would not have been killed and would not now be mourned by parents, brothers, sisters, and widows. . . . I have settled all that with God, however.
—OTTO VON BISMARCK
in 1877

EMPIRE OF GREAT BRITAIN.
AREA, 8,990,211 Sq. M.

GERMAN EMPIRE.
AREA, 210,161 Sq. M.

colonies — because it would then need a large navy to protect them.

Bismarck needed the support of these special interests. He also hoped to undermine the political position of his enemy, Crown Prince Friedrich, who was opposed to imperialism — the building of empires. If a colonial policy created conflicts with Britain, Bismarck believed that the German people would side with him against the pro-British prince and his English wife. "All this colonial business is a sham," Bismarck admitted, "but we need it for the elections."

In 1884 and 1885 Bismarck laid the cornerstone of the German colonial empire by establishing colonies in what would be known as German Southwest Africa (today known as Namibia), Togoland (a portion of which is now part of Ghana; the remainder is the independent republic of Ghana), and the Cameroons (today part of Cameroon and Nigeria) in

A cartoon satirizing British and German colonial expansionism. Bismarck had little interest in establishing colonial settlements in Africa, but in order to appease influential Germans with economic interests in colonial expansion, Bismarck claimed several African regions in 1884 and 1885.

western Africa, German New Guinea (the northeast portion of the island of New Guinea and some nearby islands), and German East Africa (roughly equal to what is now Tanzania).

Compared with the vast British and French empires, it was hardly an impressive collection of territories. What little trade Germany enjoyed with its colonies was far outweighed by the cost of protecting and administering them. Another problem was that Germany had now succeeded in antagonizing the British, who saw the new German outposts as threats to their own colonies and trade routes.

Having acquired his empire, Bismarck promptly lost interest in it. He was far more concerned with the troublesome Balkan region. In 1879 Alexander II of Russia had placed his nephew, Alexander of Battenberg, on the Bulgarian throne, fully expecting that the prince would follow Russian orders. But Alexander asserted his independence and was soon embroiled in a running feud with his Russian patrons. In 1883 Battenberg scored what appeared to be a great triumph in that struggle. He became engaged to Princess Victoria of Prussia, the daughter of Crown Prince Friedrich and the granddaughter of Britain's Queen Victoria. With such a marriage, Alexander would indeed have powerful allies.

For precisely that reason, the engagement was bitterly opposed by the Russians and Bismarck. He knew that if Germany in any way aided the unruly Battenberg, Russia might quit the Three Emperors' League in a huff and reach an understanding with France, an alliance Bismarck dreaded.

The engagement provoked a treacherous battle within the Prussian royal family. The crown princess, who enthusiastically supported the match, confronted Bismarck, who threatened to resign if the marriage took place. After one explosive shouting match the crown princess left the room in tears, crying, "You will be the death of my poor child!" "I cannot plunge my country into war on account of your ambitions!" Bismarck snapped. By March 1884 the chancellor had browbeaten Kaiser Wilhelm into forbidding the marriage.

In August 1886 the Russians had Battenberg kidnapped and removed from the throne, but the Bulgarians would not replace him with Alexander III's nominee. The Russians became convinced that Germany and Austria-Hungary were plotting to destroy their dominant role in the Balkans. The tsar refused to renew the Three Emperors' League, which was due to expire in June 1887. Now the Russians were seriously considering an alliance with France, where there was growing public enthusiasm for a war of revenge against Germany.

In one last whirlwind of political maneuvering, Bismarck managed to checkmate his adversaries at home and abroad. Using the threat of war as a pretext, he asked the Reichstag to increase the size of the army and pass a new seven-year military budget. When the budget was voted down, Bismarck called for new elections to be held in February 1887 and whipped up a campaign of patriotic hysteria. His machinations worked: his supporters won a landslide victory.

Now Bismarck moved quickly to repair his crumbling diplomatic system. On February 20 he renewed the Triple Alliance with Austria-Hungary and Italy. Russia proved more difficult to deal with, as it would not be a party to any alliance that included Austria. By June 18 Bismarck managed to conclude a bilateral Reinsurance Treaty with Russia. Each promised neutrality if the other fought a war with a third power, unless Germany attacked France or Russia attacked Austria-Hungary. The pact was signed just in time, for a month later the Bulgarians named a German prince, Ferdinand of Saxe-Coburg, as their ruler. The Russians were outraged. If they had not been bound by the Reinsurance Treaty, they might have joined an alliance with France.

The treaties of 1887 provide a fine illustration of Bismarck's political shrewdness. In the Reinsurance Treaty he won Russian friendship by secretly pledging his support if the tsar tried to capture Constantinople and the Dardanelles. But during the previous March Bismarck had already made sure

> *Despotism is the essence of his being.*
> —CROWN PRINCESS VICTORIA on Bismarck

Bismarck in 1894. Understanding that France remained embittered toward Germany after the Franco-Prussian War, Bismarck took great care in the years following to isolate France and deny it any powerful alliances. His efforts backfired, however, and by that year France and Russia had established close economic ties.

that the Russians would never attempt any such thing by secretly persuading Austria-Hungary, Britain, and Italy to promise that they would resist any attack on the Ottoman Empire. He created a masterpiece of balanced diplomacy.

The Russian government had been restricting foreign trade and foreign ownership of land in Russia. Some German landlords and merchants were hurt by this policy. German newspapers soon portrayed the tsar as a villain. Bismarck rashly supported this anti-Russian agitation, and then, on November 10, 1887, he delivered the crowning insult. While the tsar was visiting Berlin in 1887, Bismarck effectively halted German loans to Russia. Three months later the chancellor asked the Reichstag to add 750,000 men to the army, further provoking the Russians. "We no longer ask for love, either from France or from Russia. We run after nobody," Bismarck told the Reichstag. "We Germans fear God and nothing else on earth!" After working so hard for a Russian alliance, Bismarck had thoughtlessly thrown it away over a minor disagreement.

The German people applauded this bombast, but Bismarck's "financial war" backfired. Russia obtained a loan of 500 million francs from France — some of which was used to construct Russian military railroads near the German border. Within a few years, France was the largest foreign investor in Russia. The two nations, so different in their political systems, were brought together by close economic ties. In 1894 they concluded a military alliance, each promising to aid the other in the event of a German attack. Bismarck lived to see his worst nightmare come true — Germany was hemmed in by enemies from the east and the west.

8

Dropping the Pilot

On March 9, 1888, with tears in his eyes, Bismarck announced the death of Kaiser Wilhelm I to the Reichstag. Wilhelm's son became Kaiser Friedrich III, but he would reign for only 99 days. Even at the funeral Bismarck already knew that his most powerful political enemy was dying of throat cancer.

On his deathbed Friedrich tried to reconcile the chancellor and his wife by silently pressing their hands together. "Your Majesty can be assured that I shall never forget that Her Majesty is my queen," Bismarck solemnly vowed. But in fact, he immediately forgot both of them, neither bothering to attend Friedrich's funeral nor to express his condolences to the widowed Victoria.

Friedrich was succeeded by his son, Wilhelm II. The new emperor was just under 30, brash, impulsive, and not very responsible but determined to rule. Bismarck underestimated him. After Friedrich's funeral, the chancellor spent most of his time away from Berlin, confident that he could manage Wilhelm at long distance. "He makes so many enemies he doesn't need friends," Bismarck joked.

History is simply a piece of paper covered with print; the main thing is still to make history, not to write it.
—OTTO VON BISMARCK

A portrait of Bismarck by Franz von Lenbach. By 1890 Bismarck's relations with the new kaiser, Wilhelm II, were so strained that he was forced to submit his resignation. He retired to his estate, where he wrote his memoirs, showering praise on his own past achievements and criticizing his old enemies.

Friedrich III became kaiser upon the death of his father, Wilhelm I, in 1888 but only reigned for 99 days. He developed throat cancer and was succeeded by his son, Wilhelm II.

His inexperience can lead to no good. He is much too conceited. He is simply longing with his whole heart to be rid of me in order that he may govern alone (with his own genius) and cover himself with glory.
—OTTO VON BISMARCK
on Wilhelm II

In reality, Wilhelm was surrounding himself with powerful friends — military men, industrialists, and several of Bismarck's former subordinates. "I'll give the old man six months before I take complete charge," Wilhelm bragged. "There is only one master in this country, and I am it!"

Bismarck wanted to crack down once again on the socialists, whom he still regarded as violent rebels. Wilhelm opposed him. The young emperor talked of winning over the workers with wage reforms and old-age pensions. Bismarck knew such programs would be popular and tried to seize recognition for them himself. Portraying such government-sponsored reforms as truly conservative programs, he demanded restoring the antisocialist laws. In the 1890 Reichstag elections the chancellor tried to frighten the voters by conjuring up the old bogey of the reichsfeinde, evil forces threatening the empire. With the "social peril" (the socialists) everywhere, the kaiser would have to step aside and allow the elderly Bismarck to act as dictator. Contrary to Bismarck's expectations, his support in the Reichstag plummeted from 220 to 135 seats. The Social Democrats, meanwhile, garnered more votes than any other party.

Bismarck's political position was now fatally weakened. In a last-ditch effort to retain power, he tried to win the support of his old adversary, the Center party, to no avail. "I come from the political deathbed of a great man," said the Center party leader as he left the chancellory.

Two days later, on March 15, 1890, Wilhelm sent Bismarck a note demanding an appointment the following morning. Bismarck was still asleep when Wilhelm arrived, and the emperor was kept waiting for some time. When the chancellor finally appeared, he claimed that he had not seen Wilhelm's note. Furious, Wilhelm denounced Bismarck for plotting with the Center party behind his back. "The power of my sovereign stops at the door of my wife's drawing room," the chancellor coolly replied.

The conversation grew increasingly heated. Then, apparently by accident, Bismarck dropped a file of diplomatic reports in front of the emperor. Wilhelm asked to read them; the chancellor cautioned him not to. The emperor grabbed one of the papers, where he read that Alexander III of Russia had described him as a spoiled and temperamental little boy. Clearly, Bismarck meant Wilhelm to see that. If he could no longer be chancellor, then he would go down flinging a final insult in the face of his emperor.

An 1890 cartoon from the British satirical magazine *Punch* portraying the dismissal of Bismarck. Wilhelm II had to ask twice for Bismarck's resignation before he would tender it.

Kaiser Wilhelm II. While in retirement Bismarck published anonymous letters in a Hamburg newspaper attacking the foreign policy of the young kaiser. Later, the kaiser would be forced into exile when, in 1918, the government passed into the hands of the socialists.

Bismarck was a destroyer and a creator in grand style; certainly not a pure blessing for his people, but one of those powerful personalities that fate is only accustomed to employ when it desires to achieve greatness.

—THEODOR BARTH
Liberal member of
the Reichstag

Wilhelm had to demand Bismarck's resignation twice before it was finally handed over. The emperor offered his retired servant a grant and made him duke of Lauenburg. Bismarck declined the money and disdained the dukedom. "I hope everyone will continue to address me as Bismarck," he said. "I shall use the title only when traveling incognito." On March 29, escorted by a military band and a ceremonial guard, he boarded the train for Varzin. "A state funeral with full honors," he sourly remarked.

Bismarck was now 75, but he insisted, "I feel young, far too young to do nothing." He had always complained about the pressures of diplomacy, but he could not tolerate retirement. "I was used to politics," he said with a sigh, "now I miss them." For the remaining eight years of his life he languished on his estates. He dictated a couple of volumes of memoirs, always praising his own policies and striking back at his enemies. In 1891 he was elected to the Reichstag, but he never took his seat.

At first Bismarck convinced himself that Wilhelm would soon call him back to Berlin. When no imperial summons arrived, he grew bitter. He published anonymous articles in a Hamburg newspaper attacking the foreign policy of the kaiser and his ministers. Bismarck could not even bear to look at the monarch's face on German coins. Wilhelm visited him occasionally, mainly "to see how long the old man will last," but the emperor was careful not to talk politics.

Johanna died in November 1894. The following April, the cities and universities of Germany joined in a public celebration of Bismarck's 80th birthday. In a final grand gesture, Bismarck accepted the acclaim in military uniform. "The best in me and my actions has always been the Prussian officer," he proclaimed. Wilhelm paid him only a grudging compliment: "We honor today the officer, not the statesman." In the Reichstag there was a motion to send a message of congratulations, but all the enemies that Bismarck had made over the years — the liberals, the Center party, and the socialists — voted it down.

On the evening of July 30, 1898, Bismarck died in bed at Friedrichsruh. Following his orders, his tombstone read: "A true German servant of Kaiser Wilhelm I." There was no mention of Wilhelm II.

The previous autumn, Bismarck had offered his final piece of political advice to Admiral Alfred von Tirpitz. The admiral was agitating for a larger German fleet that would challenge the British navy, but Bismarck knew that such a provocation could lead to war. "Germany should keep within her frontiers," he had warned.

Already Bismarck's delicate web of diplomacy was coming unstrung. Unlike the old master, Wilhelm

A cartoon portraying Bismarck as "the last of the great trio" raises the question of the Bismarck legacy. One German historian said of Bismarck that he "left Germany with a taste for hero worship and with a tradition of political opportunism and of the unprincipled use of force."

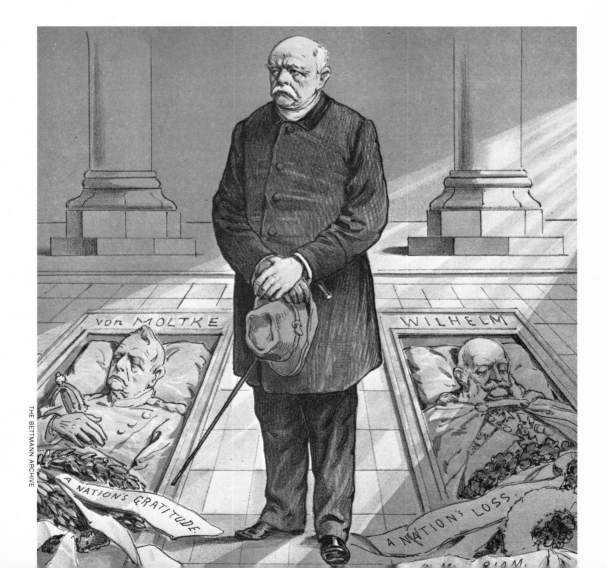

Bismarck, in military uniform, is honored at the imperial castle in Berlin as Germany celebrates his 80th birthday. The Reichstag, however, voted down a motion to send the retired chancellor a formal message of congratulations.

No man should die before having smoked one thousand cigars and drunk five thousand bottles of champagne.
—OTTO VON BISMARCK

II had little understanding of realpolitik and did not know where to stop. He built Tirpitz's navy and then recklessly confronted the other European powers in Africa. By 1907 he had frightened Britain, France, and Russia into an alliance. Bismarck had always conquered his adversaries by dividing them among themselves, playing one off against the other. While he was chancellor, Bismarck made sure that such an unstable balance of power never developed. He saw to it that France remained friendless. Although Bismarck did annoy Britain, he did not provoke it into turning against Germany, and he cleverly bound the other European powers in a network of agreements that ensured the peace.

No major war had been fought in Europe from 1871 to 1914, and Bismarck deserves much of the credit for that long interval of peace. World War I finally erupted in 1914 largely because Europe had split into two rival camps: the Triple Alliance of Germany, Austria-Hungary, and Italy versus the Triple Entente of Britain, France, and Russia. By November 1918 the empire that Bismarck had built was in ruins. Wilhelm II fled into exile, and the government passed into the hands of Bismarck's bitterest adversaries, the socialists. The victorious allies stripped Germany of her colonies, much of her home territory, and Alsace-Lorraine.

Bismarck had foreseen it all just before he died. After his last meeting with Wilhelm II, he predicted, "The crash will come twenty years after my departure if things go on like this."

The Bismarck memorial statue in Hamburg, Germany. Near the end of his life Bismarck said in his own defense: "Sometimes one may rule liberally, and sometimes dictatorially, there are no eternal rules. My only aim has been the creation and consolidation of Germany."

Further Reading

Craig, Gordon. *Germany, 1866–1945.* Oxford: Clarendon Press, 1978.

Crankshaw, Edward. *Bismarck.* New York: Viking Press, 1981.

Eyck, Erich. *Bismarck and the German Empire.* London: George Allen & Unwin Ltd., 1958.

Rich, Norman. *The Age of Nationalism and Reform, 1850–1890.* New York: W. W. Norton, 1977.

Snyder, Louis L. *Blood and Iron Chancellor.* Princeton: D. Van Nostrand, 1967.

Stern, Fritz. *Gold and Iron: Bismarck, Bleichröder, and the Building of the German Empire.* New York: Alfred A. Knopf, 1977.

Taylor, A. J. P. *Bismarck: The Man and the Statesman.* New York: Alfred A. Knopf, 1955.

Waller, Bruce. *Bismarck.* New York: Basil Blackwell, 1985.

Chronology

April 1, 1815	Otto Eduard Leopold von Bismarck born in Brandenburg, Prussia
1832	Enrolls at the University of Göttingen
1835	Graduates from the University of Berlin with a law degree
1835–39	Serves in the Prussian civil service
1847	Elected to the Prussian United Diet Marries Johanna von Puttkamer
1848	Unsuccessful revolution in Germany
April 1851	Bismarck appointed Prussian ambassador to the Bundestag
1853–56	Crimean War
1859	Bismarck appointed ambassador to Russia
Sept. 1862	Appointed Prussian prime minister
1864	Bismarck annexes Schleswig-Holstein, provoking a war with Denmark
1866	Seven Weeks' War between Prussia and Austria
1867	Bismarck appointed federal chancellor of the newly founded North German Confederation
July 1870	Franco-Prussian War begins
Jan. 18, 1871	Wilhelm I is proclaimed emperor of Germany
Feb. 1871	Bismarck negotiates French surrender
March 21, 1871	Appointed imperial chancellor
Oct. 22, 1873	Germany, Austria, and Russia form the Three Emperors' League
June–July 1878	Bismarck presides at the Congress of Berlin
Oct. 21, 1878	Reichstag enacts Bismarck's antisocialist law
1881	Bismarck proposes his social welfare program
May 20, 1882	Germany, Austria-Hungary, and Italy form the Triple Alliance
1884	Germany begins acquiring African colonies
June 18, 1887	Russia and Germany sign bilateral Reinsurance Treaty
Nov. 1887	Bismarck's "financial war" ruptures German-Russian alliance
March 9, 1888	Kaiser Wilhelm I dies; accession of Friedrich III
June 15, 1888	Friedrich III dies; accession of Wilhelm II
March 1890	Wilhelm II forces Bismarck to resign his post as imperial chancellor
July 30, 1898	Bismarck dies at Friedrichsruh

Index

Jonathan Rose teaches history at Drew University. He is a frequent contributor to *Scholastic Update* magazine, and has reviewed books for the *Wall Street Journal*, *The New York Times*, *Newsday*, and *British Heritage*. His book *The Edwardian Temperament 1895–1919* was published in 1985 by the Ohio University Press.

Arthur M. Schlesinger, jr., taught history at Harvard for many years and is currently Albert Schweitzer Professor of the Humanities at City University of New York. He is the author of numerous highly praised works in American history and has twice been awarded the Pulitzer Prize. He served in the White House as special assistant to Presidents Kennedy and Johnson.